Contents

	Acknowledgments	2
	Preface	5
1	Origins and Echoes	9
2	Getting Started	13
3	First Tracks and Beyond	19
4	State of the Skate	43
5	Downhill	63
6	Telemark Skiing	95
7	Equipment	115
8	Waxing and Prepping	139
9	Skiing with Elves and Elders	157
10	Racing and Training	167
11	Cold-Weather Smarts	177
12	Backcountry Skiing	195
13	Adventure Skiing with Ned Gillette	225
	Index	236

Preface

*E*xcept for the Olympics or World Championships, the Holmenkollen in Oslo, Norway, is the most prestigious ski competition on the year's calendar. Fifty thousand spectators arrange themselves to shout frenzied encouragement along the fifty-kilometer cross-country race course. To win is to reach the top of international racing. To participate was a dream realized for Ned Gillette on his first trip to Europe. At the sixth feeding station, manned by then U.S. team coach John Caldwell, the track was downhill just enough to keep Ned gliding. Skiing through a corridor of vocal Norwegians, who surely discerned that his inexperienced body was beginning to burn out, he eagerly took the cup of energy-laden liquid from John's extended hand. With a sweeping motion worthy of a champion beer chugger, he reared back, the better to throw the drink directly down. Too far! One ski was launched into the air, sweeping above his head as he, like a drunk slowly crumbling, landed neatly on his rear in front of his first international audience.

Since that flamboyant buttocks arrest in 1968, Ned has tried the strict business world, but skis kept appearing under his desk. He directed ski schools in California, Colorado, and Vermont; then pioneered adventure skiing expeditions on all seven continents. Skiing became serious enjoyment.

But it was the recurring memory of the Holmenkollen crumple—humorous in retrospect but devastating to young pride at the time—that caused him to consider adding another book on cross-country skiing to those already on the shelves. Why another one? It seemed to him that other books assume

Start of the American Birkebeiner, Cable, Wisconsin.

Cross-country is more than skiing on the flat.

you'll take the nourishment they offer in one neat gulp. His experience teaching, racing, and backcountry skiing suggests that the nourishment often goes over the shoulder or down the chest, or that the skier becomes airborne in the process of getting it down. He has yet to find a book fully realizing that, as his colleague John Dostal says, "When you take technique off the page and onto the snow, it can be a pretty messy process."

Along with descriptions and demonstrations of competent skiing, you'll find in the pages that follow as much on what can go wrong and what to do about it as what is right, and some exercises and suggestions on how to get a feel for the maneuvers. In short, here is information not just on ideal execution but what you'll really need to know to be comfortable on your skis and clever on the trail, whether it is a touring-center track, an alpine slope, a marathon race course, or a backcountry trek.

As at Holmenkollen, another offer of energy-laden aid was eagerly accepted, this time more successfully... this time from John Dostal. Thus did the writing of this book become a happy collaboration between one trained in skiing who took to writing and one trained in writing who took to skiing—a collaboration that came out of the teaching of skiing, by two who have been directors of one of the country's largest ski centers and ski schools.

Between the first edition of this book, nine years ago, and the second, four years later, cross-country skiing evolved steadily. Skiers attacked dramatic terrain with cross-country gear. The telemark uprising turned into a revolution. Racing times continued to drop, and we saw the first of a new technique, the marathon skate. The kind of skis once reserved in racing rooms for elite competitors began to fill retail racks. Skis with metal edges were re-designed for the demands of steeper skiing. New waxes were brewed with abandon, and waxless skis became better performers.

In the five years since the second edition, there's been no slackening in the pace of cross-country skiing's development. Not with more kids and older folks more involved than ever. Not with the new perspectives brought to the sport by alpine skiers crossing over. (Downhill and cross-country skis side by side on racks of cars used to be a gratifying but rare sight; now it's routine.) And not with the astonishing changes launched by skating. No one had to tie us to chairs to write about it.

This isn't a book on any one of these. Nor is this edition a waxing manual, a tome on equipment, or a tract on the physiology of training. As cross-country skiing has grown, so have the number of books on single aspects of it. We continue to keep cross-country between two covers because we believe that those who enjoy cross-country most are complete skiers, not tied to the tracks nor bound to the backcountry, but ready for either, depending on the progress of a winter's conditions. We continue to try to offer an overview based on situations more than theory. We think you can become a deft waxer without a degree in chemistry and pick up skating's movements without resorting to vector analysis. Furthermore, techniques are interrelated: the way your knee lines up over your foot for maximum glide when you're riding a racing ski in a fast track is the way your knee lines up over your foot for grip while making a steep traverse on climbing skins in the backcountry. The same skate that takes you through a marathon takes you across high mountain plateaus with a backpack on spring corn snow.

Much of this book is about technique. The discussion emphasizes real situations and practical advice rather than theory and prescription. Drawing on our teaching and skiing experience, we also show a variety of skiers in a variety of snows and terrain—all to the end of supple skiing.

CHAPTER 1

Origins and Echoes

When Ned Gillette visited Manchuria in 1980, he taught skiing to Chinese youngsters who still happily used handcarved wooden skis and had never seen wax. It was evident how far skiing had come in North America. This real-life skiing museum brought back thoughts on the origins of skiing.

A Stone Age carving discovered in a Norwegian cave north of the Arctic Circle shows a stick figure riding long skis in the pursuit of elk. Date: 2,000 B.C. Written reference to *skridfinnar* (sliding Finns) was made by Procopius (526–559 A.D.). Norsemen used skis in early times to travel, hunt, and fight. Often skis were of unequal length: a short one with fur fixed to the bottom for grip, and a long one on the other foot for glide. Balancing with a single pole, a skier could scooter over the rolling terrain of the Scandinavian countries. (Alpine skiing later was developed in the Alps, enabling local people to negotiate the steep mountainous slopes of Central Europe.)

As early as 1200 A.D., during the Battle of Oslo, King Sverre of Norway sent ski-equipped scouts on extensive reconnaissance missions. The scouts were called birchlegs because of their custom of wrapping their legs in bark to protect against cold.

As the hardships of life in northern climates eased, skiing evolved away from strict utilitarian purposes toward sport. In 1779 a Danish priest, Father Nicolay Jonge, mentioned that, "In Norway, it is common for kids to practice skiing so extensively that even along the coast of Norway, where there is no practical need for them, skis are used for fun." Skiing was on the way to

Kahiltna Glacier, Mt. McKinley

Equipment has changed a lot since these skis.

being the national sport of Norway.

The flowering of skiing as a sport was given impetus by two remarkable Norwegians who broke with tradition. The first was Sondre Norheim, the best skier in the Telemark district. He and his country boys dominated ski competitions in Christiania (now Oslo) starting in 1868. How? They had superior technique bolstered by innovative equipment, which gave a whole new appearance to the young sport.

Norheim hit upon the idea of a binding that much improved steering control. In addition to the old toe strap, he used twisted birch roots around his heel to give a rigid, binding connection to the ski. This was the first modern binding. It gave him the ability to do precise turns of linked beauty. Going further with his improvements, he moved another step closer to modern skiing by building the first pair of skis with side cut. Light enough to bend during the force of a turn, the maneuverable skis allowed real carved turns.

On the slopes, Norheim developed the telemark turn, which further eliminated skidding during turns. With his controlled, elegant S-turns he outskied all contestants at the Christiania meets, even at forty-two years of age. Newspapers trumpeted, "Sondre Norheim could come down like lightning and suddenly stop in a second.... a new era has arisen in skiing."

This new era was dramatized by Fridtjof Nansen's celebrated crossing of Greenland in 1888. It was a bold, pioneering step, pointing out the dependable use of skis in conquering the most inhospitable regions of the earth. The expedition took forty days. On skis, Nansen's team dragged sledges over the height of the ice cap and covered five hundred kilometers. In 1911 another Norwegian explorer, Roald Amundsen, skied to the South Pole. His relatively easy trek emphasized the tremendous advantages of gliding over snow.

Closer to home, Norwegian immigrants brought skiing to North America in the mid-1800s. The most famous of these Americanized Norsemen was Snowshoe Thompson, originally from the Telemark district. During the 1850s Snowshoe carried mail over the crest of California's Sierra Nevada for the hefty fee of two dollars per letter. As communication grew, so did his loads, often nearing one hundred pounds. The ninety-mile trip took three days to the east, but only two days on the return, due to long downhill slopes.

He was not the only "plankhopper." Fierce ski competitions erupted throughout the gold camps of the Sierra, and big money was wagered on rocketing schusses. It is said that one daredevil plummeted downhill at eighty-eight miles an hour. Cross-country skiing as utilitarian travel and exhilarating sport was here to stay.

CHAPTER 2

Getting Started

We've heard many observers of cross-country (particularly those of a downhill persuasion) say that it is a monotonous, dull, plodding sport. If you only walk on skis, it may be. But once you get the feeling of momentum carrying you down the trail, of being up and over your skis, of gentle and secure forward speed, it is a totally new sport with a subtle, gravity-defying fluidity: the more speed, the greater sense of release—even true on uphills where, with a little extra effort, you can scamper rather than plod.

To get that feeling, it's important to secure a good environment for learning. If you attempt to learn in heavy unbroken snow, you'll have a hard time getting into a smooth glide. And icy, rutted snow demands a degree of control of your skis that you need time to develop.

Ski areas now routinely groom their trails and teaching tracks (with the same sort of machines used in downhill ski areas) to a level that is sufficient for international competition. (That's why groomers will grimace when asked, "Do I just put my skis in these ruts." And why they charge a fee for skiing.) As for the ice and crust, a bristling array of harrows, tillers, scarifiers, and powdermakers can chew it up, leaving behind a finely granulated and eminently skiable surface. A decade ago, freeze-thaw conditions would have armored trails to the extent that only experts with an appetite for a rattling wild ride would use them.

Learning on groomed snow makes it easier to develop proper technique. Instructors use groomed snow as a comfort zone, along with appropriate terrain: easy ups and downs.

Cross-country can be as social as you like, or as solitary.

Crack track packers and skating surface specialists at work

When you're on your own, work within that comfort zone, steadily trying to expand its borders. This is especially true for downhill. Take a few runs on a nonintimidating hill—steep enough for comfortable sliding and easy turns. After a while, speed is not as scary, and everything seems to slow down; you have plenty of time to turn. As this happens, you no longer merely hang on; you look ahead and anticipate how you can maintain or even increase your speed, you move farther up the hill, or you find a slightly steeper one.

Along the way, don't let your more experienced friends "sandbag" you, taking you touring on terrain that is beyond your developing abilities. These beat-outs generally involve downhills that are hard on body and spirit. Be game enough to expand the comfort zone, but resist when you must.

Whether you're learning from a book or an instructor, don't create mental obstacles that will get in the way of surmounting the physical ones. Occasionally students introduce themselves to their instructors by announcing, "I want you to know that you're dealing with a klutz." For these people and for the instructor there is heavy psychological weather ahead. It is not very helpful at the beginning of a lesson to get down on yourself. This will only short-circuit your progress. So will competing with other students or your instructor, or assuming that you can learn all of cross-country skiing in a day, or concentrating on your failures and forgetting your successes.

A successful businessman from New York, outfitted with the latest racing gear, expected to become an expert skier in a week of intensive instruction. His expectations so greatly exceeded what was possible in the time he had given himself that he became unwittingly unreceptive to learning and made little progress, which led to an acute case of frustration. His problem was compounded by a sense of always being on display. When we were out skiing together, as soon as another instructor approached he promptly fell off his skis, probably thinking, "There's another one who is going to see how poorly I ski!" The second instructor had no idea that he had been called for jury duty. To help our student understand the bind he had put himself in, we asked if he could make us shrewd and successful investment bankers in the same time period.

For many skiers the words "falling" and "failing" not only sound alike but equal each other. As soon as backside touches snow, the self-indictment begins. Much better to remember that snow is nontoxic, and try to focus on *why* you fell: look at the track your ski made, remember where you were looking or where your hands were. Students who have fallen on downhills will often be asked by an instructor, "Where were your hands?" Often a quick, protective, "In the wrong place," is the response. But what the instructor is after is physical focusing, not psychological judgment. The skier who is relaxed enough to say, "It felt as if they got behind me," is making an important discovery about skiing. If good skiers were to get down on themselves every time they took a windmilling half gainer at high speeds, they'd be too depressed to wax their skis for another day's run!

Another day's run (call it insightful repetition) is just what is needed. You don't have to be in a class to tune up your skiing. You just have to be willing to go back over the section of trail that threw you, practicing and changing your approach until you have mastered it. "You make it look so easy. I feel sort of

Work within your comfort zone, allowing for the odd act of bravado.

unbalanced being on one ski at a time," says the despairing student to the instructor, who may ski daily and take an off-season vacation on skis. "And why not?" replies the instructor. "You've been on skis for all of ten minutes." Remember the first time you drove an automobile? Was your timing a bit shaky in traffic? So too in learning to ski: there is simply no substitute for getting kilometers under your skis. And you have to prevent your expectations from boiling over while you're accumulating the distance, perfecting your technique so you feel comfortable on your boards in all trail conditions and instinctively do things right. How do you eat an elephant? One bite at a time.

Progress is relative. Getting a little jogging glide on the flats may provide the beginning or casual skier with all the speed desired, while the marathon foot runner aspiring to equal past road-running times will be striving for much more, as will the alpine racer who tries to carve high-speed turns on skinny skis and the hard-core backpacker who wants to trek through the wilderness in winter. Levels of expertise must be measured by your own standards. What is possible for one skier may not be for another, and expectations that are now beyond reach only lead to frustration. Not being able to do a parallel turn doesn't mean you cannot have fun on cross-country skis. Also, it's remarkable how agile and coordinated everyone is in some aspect of skiing. One woman was distressed that she couldn't learn to snowplow as fast as others in her class. She had to be reminded that, if she wanted to keep score, she was at the head of the class in skiing uphill.

It is useful, occasionally, to take things apart and monitor your skills as you ski. Think of it as a checklist or tune-up. Take things one at a time, focusing on hands, body position, leg movement, and so forth.

CHAPTER 3

First Tracks
and Beyond

*T*he skier stretched out in a stride has long been cross-country skiing's emblem. To that has been added the skater's powerful sway. But most people getting acquainted with cross-country skiing will work from what's familiar: putting one foot in front of the other. Most but not all. Cross-country skiing is a sliding, gliding sport. Downhill skiers are already familiar with those sensations. They've been coming to cross-country skiing in ever greater numbers recently, and for them, we're offering another way to get going on cross-country skis (see Learning to Cross-Country Ski: An Approach for Downhill Skiers). So consider this chapter a menu. Stay and stride or move on and return.

Striding

The *diagonal* stride, with its long axis of opposite arm and leg, starts with a walk. We've long heard the sport promoted with the slogan "if you can walk you can ski." Walking is where it should start, but for some skiers that's where it ends. Some skiers stay resolutely upright, never getting beyond a ponderous shuffle, never getting that glide. How to get it? Change your posture. Slump to begin to stride. In short, more gorilla for more glide.

The biomechanics are inescapable: hunch over, round your back, and you'll turn walking into gliding. Moreover, you

It happens (here) in Sun Valley; it can happen anywhere there's snow. . . .

More gorilla for more glide

will feel more secure and less wobbly on your skis.

Now begin to jog on your skis. It's like springing across a stream. Commit your whole body to the forward effort, and you land not on the jogger's asphalt road but on a platform sliding on the snow. Stay hunched over and that platform won't slide out from under you.

We've left you balancing on one foot gliding along. How do you obtain a grip in this slippery stuff to continue jogging? A rubber sole is secure on asphalt in the summer, but what about these skis?

Listen to a seven-year-old explaining things to an obvious first timer: "See, all you have to do is put a little pressure on your skis as you go forward." Here in one short sentence of simplicity and sophistication is the essence of diagonal striding.

This pressure is called kick. When your weight is on the forward, gliding ski, press (kick) down on it, so it will grip the snow and provide a platform from which to launch yourself onto the other ski, which is coming forward—a skier's form of jogging. Many beginners think that what makes you move forward is only a "scootering" or pushing back with one ski, but you need to press down for grip first. Think of how you would jog on a slippery, snow-covered road, pressing down when your weight is directly over your forward or kicking foot for maximum traction.

Now try to put it all together, jogging with a steady rhythm. Avoid any distinct hesitation at the end of each stride. You don't "freeze" at the end of each stride as you run down the street, do you? A good way to feel this rhythm is to follow a good skier who is skiing slowly, matching strides. Or try jogging up a moderate hill as if you didn't have skis on. This will speed up your rhythm to a point where you can't think every segment of your stride through to needless complication and will give you security if you're worried about catapulting over the tips of your skis. It's also an antidote for those who are preoccupied with trying to remember which hand comes forward with which leg. (Your body's been doing it for how many years now? The addition of skis and poles is not going to make a difference.)

Mass and motion: As your skiing develops, you'll naturally look around at other skiers. The best will seem to be windmilling smoothly. To see how they're getting so much seemingly effortless glide, take a suggestion from Dick Taylor, formerly of the U.S. Ski Team staff, and look *through* those waving extremities to the mass of the skier. A good skier's mass

First-time cross-country skiing is not all that different from jogging.

Learning to Cross-Country Ski:
An Approach for Downhill Skiers

Perhaps you are an alpine or downhill skier who is taking a day off from lift-served skiing. Maybe the lifts have shut down due to wind, or your knees are screaming for a rest from pounding bumps. Maybe you've always been curious about cross-country skiing. Whatever, a day of *skiing* is not going to be sacrificed. So you go to a cross-country ski area.

First you rent equipment. You get waxless skis with a patterned base for grip (the most convenient ski for ski areas to rent: they don't have to hassle with waxing the skis, taking the chance they might not get it right, and then clean them up). One thing about waxless skis, they don't, by their very design, glide well. Certainly not like a downhill ski.

After a hesitant or uncomfortable question or two about how cross-country skiing is actually done, you take off. Well, not exactly. You set out, but there's no lift-off. Not much glide. And after an hour or two of shuffling and trudging, you're back. Cross-country, for you at least, is awful.

It shouldn't be. Consider that if you're a downhill skier, you're that and more. You're already pretty much a cross-country skier, given the skills you have in addition to your downhill abilities. You're a glider; not only are you comfortable on a sliding ski, but you relish it enough to pay $30 a day for the privilege. You can push yourself along with your poles; sidestep up and down; herringbone hills. You can step turn and skate turn. You shuffle on the flats or skate—how else to get into a lift line? The problems are short poles that don't give much mechanical advantage on the flats and boots that lock down at the heels, making striding difficult. And cross-country centers that don't treat you as a nearly complete cross-country skier.

We suggest sliding, not shuffling, into cross-country. Start with a pair of waxable—but unwaxed—skis. (For someone with no downhill background and unfamiliar with the sensation of gliding, waxless skis may offer just enough glide.) And go a little longer with the poles, even to the top of the shoulder.

Alpine-length poles are terrible on the flats. You have to push behind you, palming the grips to get a little extra length. Recall your progress into a lift line. But with cross-country

Long poles make it easy to skate on cross-country skis.

poles, you can be up front and out front. (See Double poling and begin pushing yourself along.)

You can skate, right? It's a lot easier on cross-country equipment. (Although it took us a long while to realize it.) Start off the way you would to get to the lifts. You'll pole and skate on each side. If you're still keeping the poles way behind you, imagine that you are a puppet. As your hands come up and forward to pole, let them pull your thigh up, as if it's attached by a string. Begin to pole, then set your ski down. You're skating in downhiller's rhythm but with cross-country power. Once you're comfortable with this, try it cross-country style—poling on one side only and simply stepping back to the first side to resume poling. It's much less fatiguing, and you're still sliding along at a pretty good clip.

Throw in some step turns. You're getting used to having a free heel—the shackles are off. If there's a bit of a hill, feel how much easier a herringbone is.

Now that you've done some skating and have gotten a feel for being on one sliding ski at a time, you're ready for striding, the other way of getting around on cross-country skis. Instead of the steady sway of skating, in which the traction comes from edging your skis—but you felt that almost immediately—striding is simply that: the old familiar rhythm of jogging. Since you'll use the ski base rather than the edge for traction, at this point you had better have some grip wax put on your skis or trade them in for a pair of "waxless" skis with a mechanical gripping pattern.

So much of the downhill to cross-country transition is mental. The skills are pretty much there. Just let the free heel release them.

is centered over the skis. Cross-country skis take you for a ride. But don't ride in the back seat. Which is to say, as former ski team member, Lindsay Putnam, once put it, "Don't leave your behind behind." If you've ever ridden a wave, you know that you've got to stay out on it; get behind and you lose the ride.

Get your hips up and over the lead ski. Beginning skiers often shrewdly notice that the leg of an accomplished skier trails up and behind. It's not because that skier pushed back—we hope we've skewered that notion already—but because the hips were committed to the forward ski. If your skiing leaves you doing the splits—back foot and ski down on the track—freeze in that pose, as if in the middle of a stride. Feel the weight on both your back foot and your front. Now steadily move your hips up and forward until... lift-off! With your weight committed to that front ski, the rear is free; that commitment will put you on the fly.

If your hips aren't up and over your lead ski, you'll often hear about it—from the other ski. It's that noisy, persistent "whap" as your hips drop, and the ski that's sliding through is weighted too soon and driven into the snow. This does put you more securely on two skis, so you feel less shaky, but kills your glide. The time-worn name for this ailment is "slapping the track." Troubleshoot by taking to the stairs. First step up toddler style: right foot up, and then the left foot brought up and set down next to it. You've just slapped the stairs. Now try it up and through in the adult fashion. Feel how your hips come forward.

To get it all moving forward, it may help to imagine you're in a body cast from shin to shoulder, launching the whole unit onto the lead ski. "Tony knows," says former U.S. Ski Team coach and sometime Gillette training partner Mike Gallagher. He doesn't have a real "Tony" in mind; it's toe–knee–nose, all in a line. Be conscious of riding a vertical shin on your front leg, and try to maintain a constant angle rather than bouncing up and down. Where do you feel your weight? On your heel (good) or on your toe? With weight on the heel it's easier to maintain balance as you're riding more on the rear or tracking portion of the ski. And you can kick down with the whole foot to set wax or waxless gripping pattern.

Slippery strides: If you are slipping and not getting your skis to grip the snow, it can be for one of several reasons:

• Wrong or insufficient wax or ineffective waxless pattern.

• Too stiffly cambered skis for your technique or the snow conditions. Try a softer pair, waxed the same.

• No weight shift onto your front ski.

• Pushing only backward when you kick—what technicians call a late kick. Get an earlier and more powerful kick by starting to put pressure on your skis with your toes; imagine your boots are cleated and that you're trying to get those cleats dug right into the snow.

Poling

When you start skiing, chances are you'll be most concerned with what's going on underfoot. But coming to grips with your poles will make the biggest difference in your skiing. Take us literally, here. Maintaining a free and easy poling motion depends on how you hold the pole. Getting it right is as important—and as basic—as clipping into your bindings.

As the strap hangs down toward you, come up through and then grasp the handle so that the strap is under your hand; you're pushing down on the strap more than on the handle. Adjust the strap snugly enough that the knob at the end of the handle nestles in the crotch between your thumb and forefinger—you'll feel some pressure from the pole strap on the meaty (karate-chopping) part of your hand.

Just as a proper grip is the key to better poling, so is correct arm and poling motion a key to better skiing. The way you use your poles dictates your rhythm, body position, relaxation, and speed.

Many beginners use their poles solely as outriggers or as canes for balance. Outriggers help you stay upright but supply no push down the track. Abandon the notion of poles as training wheels. You should be working your arms vigorously, depending on the grip of your wax and the incline of the trail, to supply a good deal of your forward power.

Plant your pole (stick it into the snow) in front so it is angled backward for immediate push. Push straight down and back past your hip. Your poling motion should take place half in front and half in back of your body when skiing on the flat, or you lose much of your pushing potential.

To recover the pole, bring it forward at any angle, swinging your hand like a pendulum past your hip. Don't try to lift the pole vertically over the snow. This can lead to some pretty bizarre recovery motions, including the Swim, the Windmill, the Roundhouse, the Disposal of the Dead Mouse, and the Pattycake, all of which we've seen in teaching over the years. One thing they all have in common is lifting rather than swinging the pole forward. And that means loss of momentum and an upright rather than a forward body position.

If you're having trouble with the recovery, try skiing without poles, letting your hands pull you out over your skis and down the track. You'll have one less piece of equipment to think about. Allow your arms to swing back and forth comfortably to set your tempo, keeping your hands relatively low in front. If you can see them up in front of your face, they're too high and will throw you back off your forward ski instead of pulling you onto it.

Be definite both in planting and recovering the pole. A weak action or a super-slow rhythm will allow your pole to skip along the snow as it is coming forward and throw off your balance and timing.

With practice you'll be able to lengthen your stride and increase your speed.

If pushing the pole past your hip seems awkward, check your strap adjustment. You may be gripping the poles too tightly. Cradle the pole in your hand. Relax your fingers. For maximum thrust with a relaxed arm, release your grip on the handle as you extend back. But don't let go of the pole completely, allowing it to hang from the strap. As an arm swings forward, the snug strap pulls the pole back into the hand. Try to release the pole only with the last two fingers. This gives total extension, yet allows control of the pole action with thumb and forefinger.

For more power and efficiency, your arms should swing like pendulums from the shoulders when poling, as they do when you walk. Larger shoulder and back muscles provide more thrust than arm muscles. Shoulders that are locked force the arms to move only from the elbows, resulting in weak, choppy poling. Comfortably bent arms provide maximum power for the energy expended. Think of how you would hammer a nail. Would you hammer with arms straight or

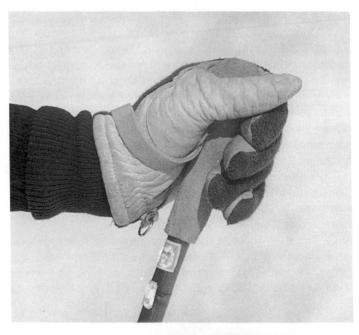

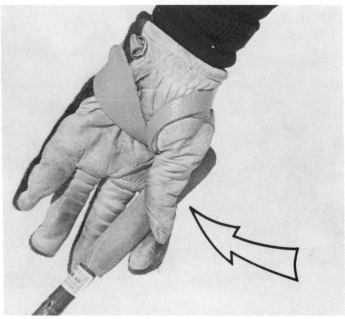

For easy poling, release your grip on the pole as you push back.

Left shoulder and side are doing plenty of work here.

slightly bent?

As you become a better skier carrying real speed down the track, your arms will lift higher, and you'll have a tremendous sensation of the swing of your arms setting your overall pace. Your whole body is drawn ahead by your arms coming through quickly. It's just like running: recall how much you work your arms when you want to move into a sprint.

Hands lifted too high in front bring your upper body back off your skis with each stride in a bobbing motion that directs much of your energy up into the air instead of down the trail. It also slows your tempo, provides only a push down into the snow instead of a push forward, and allows no push or extension of your poling behind your leg.

To get the feel of efficient poling, try this exercise. Find a slightly downhill track and push yourself along with just your poles, in an alternating rhythm. Don't use your legs, but make sure you bend your knees slightly—it's easier. Working hard? That's how much energy you should use, even when striding. Experiment to discover what is most efficient. Straighten your arms, bend them, angle your poles differently, raise your hands high or low in front, grip your poles differently. You'll soon dis-

Isolate the arms to improve your poling.

cover the most efficient means of propelling yourself. It doesn't take bulging muscles for this one, only correct technique. Once you feel it, you'll ski a new and easier way.

Power poling: A fast, efficient skier will swing the lead arm through quickly and let it pull the hips forward with it. This

A sure sign that a skier is sustaining his glide by poling early is the "separation" between poling arm (left) and recovering arm (right) as the feet are together just before kicking.

is a more vigorous movement than merely reaching forward, and it's easier if the trailing pole is fully extended. Less efficient skiers tend to stop it at the hip. Not only does this make it harder for the *other* pole to work properly, you'll lose a foot or more of extra glide or distance—like checking the swing of bat, golf club, or tennis racket. Getting the pole in the snow early lets you keep up your momentum. Don't pose with it out front; get the pole in the snow quickly and begin pushing to sustain the glide.

Double poling: It's time to give the legs a rest. Double poling does just that, and because you're balancing on two skis, it's stable. Double poling is just the thing for sections of trail that are choppy or icy. It's also easier, faster, and more efficient than diagonal striding on the flats—and especially on gradual downhills. We've long felt that most skiers don't double-pole enough when skiing prepared trails. We suspect that's partly because many skiers are on slower-gliding waxless skis. But even on waxless skis, be opportunistic. Throw in some double poling on different kinds of terrain to feel the differences in efficiency.

Since the second edition of this book, double-poling technique has changed dramatically. Thanks to the longer poles used for the new skating technique, double poling has gotten easier and more efficient, and this is just as true for the Saturday tourer as for the Sunday racer.

Double poling: lead skier straight-arming it with short poles; second skier using mechanical advantage of longer poles

Though faster plastic skis came along more than a decade ago, poles remained at their traditional to-the-armpit length. Any beginner can feel immediately that poles must be planted with a backward angle rather than a vertical one in order to push forward. And it's easier to push by compressing your upper body onto the poles, hinging at the waist, rather than just by sculling with the arms. However, with the fast skis and short poles, you had to plant the pole more vertically and farther forward, lest at high speed you slid past it. That demanded rigid, nearly locked arms. As our good friend, ski researcher Bert Kleerup, puts it, double poling was like doing the gymnast's Iron Cross exercise on the rings.

The longer poles used for skating made double poling immediately more powerful: you could start pushing with your hands higher in order to get a longer stroke and angle the poles back for immediate forward progress. Skating poles were still a little too long for the traditional striding technique, but a compromise, say an addition of ten centimeters, made for better double poling without compromising the stride.

The longer poles let you go even easier on the arms. Four years ago we noted that it was critical to keep the arms in a fixed position, angled at the elbow. With longer poles you can "preload" or stretch the powerful muscles of the sides, back, and arms like elastic bands. As you "fall" forward onto your poles (they'll hold you up), let your elbow come closer to the pole shaft, like you're starting to arm wrestle. You'll feel a smooth catch and stretch. If not, take a suggestion from coach Dick Taylor and ski "with high hands." Think about bringing your elbows forward, and the preloading should be right on schedule. The upper body compresses as in an abdominal curl. Then, like a pitcher's delivery motion, drive the poles through, finally engaging the relatively weaker arm muscles and getting a final snap.

You'll notice that your hips move slightly back. That should be natural; don't compromise the power of that compressing upper body by dropping your seat. And don't make it harder to get back up to vertical by bending over too far.

Kick double pole: Adding a kick to the straight double pole will help you keep up your momentum on slower snow or even slight uphills. The kick comes in as you swing your arms forward. With flexed legs, kick down and back. For maximum thrust, the kicking foot should start a bit ahead of the other foot.

Kick double pole. Left (kicking) foot begins slightly ahead in first photo and doesn't come through until poling begins, third photo.

You'll feel that your wax will grab a little longer, and that you can get a little more purchase this way than if your foot were farther back under your hips.

Now you've opened the scissors, as it were, gliding on one ski, body extended forward, kicking leg extended to the rear—it's that rear leg that acts as a counterbalance so you can get your upper body farther out over your poles, which yields more power. For maximum extension lean forward from the ankles, not the waist.

Begin to close the scissors, but one blade at a time; that is, plant your poles and put pressure on them just as in a double pole. Then begin to bring the trailing leg through. If it comes through too soon, it will inhibit glide and poling power. So, too, will letting your poles get too far out in front. Remember to keep them at a slight backward angle—hands ahead of baskets.

Beginners may find the kick double pole difficult to coordinate. Better, we think, to concentrate on developing a solid straight double pole. But those who aspire to racing in the traditional style will want to pick it up.

Upward Mobility

With proper technique and equipment, skiing uphill can be an easy and graceful pleasure, more cruising than hiking.

Your basic diagonal stride, with only a few modifications, will get you up hills. You won't get as much glide, so you'll have to increase your tempo and shorten your poling motion. To get maximum glide and bite from your wax, slide the lead foot a bit

Skiing a steep hill: Lead foot slides ahead of knee; arms shorten up.

more forward—as if you're pushing your heel forward. Then compress your ankle, not your knee, and roll over it for best traction.

As much attention ought to be paid to your arms as to your body position. Your arms ought to be crisply driving forward, lifting you up the hill like a high-jumper approaching the

To kick on uphills, compress and roll over ankle.

bar. There should be plenty of shoulder in your poling to bring your torso forward and give you increased leverage. On uphills, because of the slower speed and diminished glide, the arm stops near your hip to allow the quick recovery that will keep up your momentum. How close to the hip depends on how good your wax is and how steep the hill. Bad wax and a killer incline will keep hands more in front. Your arms set your tempo; if they move quickly, your legs will follow. Tired racers pole sluggishly, letting their elbows come out from their bodies, thus losing power. Remember that the arm extension in poling is like a push-up, and push-ups are harder if your hands are way out to the side.

When skiers have trouble with hills, it's usually because they straighten up at the bottom and bob up and down rather than try to slide the skis uphill. Or if they tiré, they'll hinge forward at the waist and find their skis are suddenly slippery. Simply looking up the hill will help put your weight properly on your skis. (For years native Vermonters have used the term "way bent over" to describe an extraordinarily stupid person.)

Many beginners have to develop not only the technique but the strength to ski uphill. They mix in some ski walking with their ski jogging. Or they should. Plodding up every hill won't yield results, but slowing down and walking when you have to—as long as you pay attention to technique—will. Don't straighten up and step, but slide your ski forward, feeling your weight come onto it. When the angle of the hill lessens, or when you catch your breath, get your arms moving and start skiing again.

You will get a good grip on the snow if your weight is over your kicking foot. As your foot comes forward, "hit" the ski with your heel for just an instant. This is the easiest way to achieve correct weight position: if your heel can contact the ski, your weight must be directly over that foot. Think about pushing your heel forward. Then compress your ankle and roll over it for traction.

When you're skiing uphill on tracks that are filling in with soft snow that is shearing away from the hard track underneath it, you may have to adjust the kind of pressure you put on your skis, going up "on little cat feet." It's the same kind of adjustment you'd make when running on a snowy road. If an uphill track seems slippery, you might get better traction on the packed snow off to one side.

Herringboning

When the hill becomes very steep or your wax starts to slip, it's time to break into a duck walk for extra grip.

Spread the tips of your skis far apart, keeping the tails together to form a wedge, or reverse snowplow. Tip your skis severely on their inside edges so they bite into the snow for hold. Bend your knees forward and inside. Step *forward* in this spread-eagle position in your regular ski-striding rhythm. Chop little steps in the snow with each stride. If the herringbone feels awkward, you are probably waddling uphill with your weight too far back, which may be why you're stepping on the tail of the opposite ski.

When you start slipping, break into a herringbone for more climbing power.

Try to get up the hill with as narrow a herringbone as possible. Maybe you need to spread your tips only two feet apart and use your edges to get up; no need to automatically spread them an extra couple of feet, making it more awkward.

Sidestepping

On steeper inclines, where you are hesitant about negotiating the terrain, sidestepping is the technique of last resort. It's slow and tedious, but wonderfully secure going both up and down.

Place your skis across the fall line and roll your ankles into the slope to edge your skis for grip. (The fall line is defined as a snowball's path of least resistance down the hill.) Step up or down by shifting your weight from one ski to the other. In deep snow, control your ski by lifting up with your toes and pressing down with your heel. On an icy slope, lean your body away from the slope for secure edge bite. Leaning into the hill will push your edges off the snow, often leading to a bruising slide.

You can get a good feeling for this maneuver while still on the flat. Stand on your skis, extend one arm to the side, and have a friend tug steadily, trying to pull you off balance. You'll put up maximum resistance by driving your knees away from the pull. Look down and notice that your upper body is over your feet and that your skis are automatically on their edges. This may feel scary on a steep slope as you are poised looking down a breathtaking pitch, but your driving knees and edged skis will give you a reassuring platform.

Traversing and Tacking

Instead of sidestepping straight up or down, traversing or zigzagging on a gradual angle is often an easier solution to a steep slope, especially when toting a heavy backpack. A clever route tacking around the worst obstacles is extremely efficient in deep snow or on long mountain tours where energy must be conserved.

Tacking, a slightly higher-speed version of a traverse, combines straight uphill skiing, a slight herringbone, and plenty of edging. Diagonal-stride uphill at the steepest angle you can manage that will still allow you to move quickly. Change directions by taking an uphill step off to the other side. Less tedious than the herringbone, tacking can be fast and subtle.

Kick Turning

How do you turn around at the end of each zig or zag? A kick turn will change your direction one hundred and eighty degrees. The quicker you do this little maneuver, the better your chances are of success.

Kick your lower ski forward, then around in an arc so it faces the opposite direction. You are now standing like Charlie

You don't have to be a ballet dancer to change directions. The key is flicking your foot up and over, pulling your toes toward your shin.

Chaplin, feet pointing in opposite directions. This is fourth position in ballet; but forget the plié. To hesitate is to lose. Quickly shift weight onto the ski pointed in the new direction and bring the other one around parallel. Try this one on the flat the first few times, working up to steeper terrain. When skiers have trouble with kick turns it's usually because they swivel the ski out to the side to turn it. No matter what length of ski you're on, it's still too long to turn it that way. The better way is to lift your toe and the tip of the ski straight up (you'll feel it in your shin), then flop the ski over.

On steep slopes, some skiers prefer to kick-turn facing downhill, as it's easier to get the skis free of the hill. Others prefer to turn into the hill, reckoning that if they lose it at midpoint, they'll be closer to a self-arrest position.

Tandem Skiing

"This ain't no Oslo,
This ain't no Putney.
This ain't but foolin' around."
        (with apologies to the Talking Heads)

After you've gotten it all together on your own, enlist a friend for some tandem skiing. The ardor of these two, both ski-industry luminaries, is undiminished after eight years.

CHAPTER 4

State of the Skate

You could have bet the ranch that when we suggested learning to skate, in the first edition, we meant it as no more than an aid in developing a better stride. You could have doubled down, four years later, when we said that a version of it called the marathon skate was "rapidly gaining popularity, even among citizen racers"; it was an appraisal that time would prove much too modest.

More than racers were swayed—literally—by skating. The public was charmed. "It looks so graceful," "It's like dancing" were the typical comments as skating took wing in the middle of the 1980s. Skiers were responding to a movement in cross-country that's all glide.

Like an ice skater, the skating skier is constantly pushing off a splayed, gliding ski. Now it is true that the skating skier is traveling from side to side. But in spite of this wasteful tacking, the skating skier keeps a more constant velocity. There's no pause—however momentary—when the ski stops for the grip wax or the serrated waxless pattern to engage the snow for traction, as happens in straight-ahead striding. It all adds up. Coaches and researchers were quick with the numbers: skating proved more efficient. By some reckonings, skating is a third faster than double poling, and nearly twice as fast as diagonal striding. In racing, its effect was devastating. Imagine a new way of running that would abruptly lower the world record in the marathon by twenty minutes, and you'll have an idea of the recent impact of skating.

When a skier takes to skating with the grace of this veteran, it's no wonder a Lycra lady is attracted.

Skating's for Everyone

Skating has appealed to skiers who have no fast-lane ambitions. It is the feel, for one thing—the winter waltz, the on-snow sashay, in which the swing's the thing. But beyond that there is the function. Even for recreational skiers, skating is not just for show; it's another efficient and useful way to get around. Grip wax isn't necessary, and you don't need tracks. Skating will get you going without having to find skied-in or set tracks. On a packed snowmobile trail, when your skis slide out to the side as you stride, try skating instead. And skating lets you extend the season, taking off on thin cover on a golf course or on a frozen pond that otherwise would be impossible to pack and track. In spring conditions, skating shines. When snow softens up into spring "corn," it's "go anywhere" time if you skate. Midwesterners call this "crust-country skiing." What about those days when the snow's falling right at the freezing point, and the going is tough, despite the best efforts of trail crews at ski areas and parks? Even newly set tracks quickly turn slithery and unstable, and both waxed and waxless skis alternately slip and clog with snow. It's not time to quit, it's time to skate. Skating weatherproofs a day's skiing.

If skating's made skiers less dependent on tracks, it's also let them make something more of their own tracks—and of others'. More than the incision and suture pattern in the snow that marks the forward progress of a striding skier, skating's characteristic slashes reveal impulse and edging, power and finesse. Are you getting more glide than the skier who preceded you? Working your edges more deftly? The snow tells all. And to skiing uphills skating allows a bit of the swagger of snaking an enviable set of tracks when skiing down. "You skated it?" you might hear. "The whole hill?" That's what Dostal asked his associate Jon Cowan after seeing an impressive set of tracks strung out nicely *up* the steepest downhill run on their local trail system. "Yeah, my tracks in the Chute," said Cowan, grinning with complete satisfaction. "I laced it up."

It took skiers at the elite level of competition a while to lace up skating. The technique didn't drop into skiing, it evolved, but so quickly that the atmosphere was frenetic. The Authorized Shorter Version of how skating developed maintains that American Bill Koch picked it up from Swedish marathon racers and used it to win the World Cup in 1982. But there's also been an ongoing search for the first skater, *Homo skaterus.* Doubtful we'll settle on a candidate. Skating has been around for a long time. Without it, downhill skiers could scarcely get into a lift line.

We can credit Koch for bringing skating to the fore. But questions remained to be answered before skating caught hold in cross-country technique. Skating was first used for the flats, with skis still kick-waxed for the hills. Without the kick wax you could go faster. But for as long as 30 kilometers? And what about going up steep hills? Finding answers in the middle 1980's gave cross-country the feel of a frontier town. It was a time to be savored. Few sports have experienced such dramatic change so quickly. It was as if the butterfly emerged from the breast stroke, the straddle shifted to the flop style in high-jumping, and the long fiberglass vaulting pole supplanted all others—at once in a single sport.

Skating put everyone on the same learning curve, albeit at different points. From elite skiers to interested tourers, *everyone* was working out the new style. Make that styles. One Norwegian coach suggested twelve ways to skate, laying out the ski and pole work like the foot diagrams in a manual on ballroom dancing. When it came to technique, one nationally ranked skier summed up what was happening: "I may change my mind next week." The marathon skate yielded to even faster techniques known as the V-1, followed by the V-2 or V-Square, and even the V-3, leaving some wondering if skating was outstripping its v'cabulary.

When changes came, they often did so with no respect for venue or athletic accomplishment. We've seen videotape from the 1985 races at Seefeld, Austria, showing a member of the U.S. Ski Team learning a new skate midrace. The Norwegian he was following uphill had abandoned the slower skating style of what we called the flying herringbone for a faster V-skate, double poling hard off one side. The American was flailing, his form no better than that of many beginners. And this was at the World Championships... (a major venue).

One of our skating models, Bruce Likly, learned the new skate there, too, and brought it back to the Eastern collegiate ski racing circuit, where he ate up the hills and the competition in the first race as rival coaches yelled at their skiers to do as he

Alongside the tracks there's plenty of room to skate. But which skate works best?

had done—learn a new skill on the spot. Our other model, former World Junior Champion Hanne Krogstad, recalls her disbelief that teammate Likly could ski up a whole hill this way. But then, of course, skiers tried it out, muscle groups adjusted, and the frontiers of skating were further expanded.

Should you skate? We think we've already made that case. Should you skate exclusively? For a while, that was a hot question, with range warfare between skaters and striders impending. But now things are more relaxed. Experienced skiers realize that it's worth keeping the classical or diagonal style in their repertoire for a number of reasons, variety being one of them. Diagonal striding works different muscle groups, giving others a rest from the demands of skating. It's useful; in soft, cold powder snow, the skiing is likely to be better in the tracks than in the skating lanes. And it is like everyday walking or running, while slipping out from under the full force of gravity.

Getting Started

Skating looks so inviting that you may hop out of the tracks onto the smoothly packed skating lanes to try it for your-

Brother see, brother do. Even messing around on a pair of waxless skis, the smaller one's swaying and skating.

Tower of Power: A right triangle is the key to skating right. Notice how the head lines up over the left foot and how the shoulders squared over the left ski allow the left pole to be planted for maximum thrust. Commitment to the gliding ski is the same as in the diagonal stride (see page 26, right photo).

self. Soon you begin to wonder how passing skaters make it look so easy. You'll be shocked to see the smooth bases of the skaters' skis. But that's essential—no waxless pattern or kick wax. Even better, lube the *whole* ski with glider wax instead of just tips and tails; you'll glide more easily, which will make skating less taxing. Skis specifically designed for skating are helpful but not vital, but you do need poles that may seem shockingly long compared to conventional ones. To the nose should be about right.

If you're coming to skating from striding, you'll find more similarities than you might expect. While the two styles have a different look, a different rhythm and feel, one thing doesn't change—the physics. In both skating and striding, the best skiers ride a single ski at a time. They have their hips up and over the gliding ski, keeping all the freight on the train. They maintain glide by effective use of poles, and they generate it from a forceful and well-timed push-off or kick.

We'll not present so much a teaching or learning progression as a menu for skating. We've found that skiers take to some skating styles better than others. But however you start—and in the last chapter we hope we got downhillers going with a variety of skating familiar to them—your goal should be a strong V-1 skate. It will take you across the flats and up the hills. And be-

Walking through a skate. Left ski and poles hit snow simultaneously. Poles are displaced to clear the skis. Lift of right heel shows how just this much twist pulls weight off the right and onto the left ski.

cause two poles and one ski are working together, it's as stable as a tripod.

The V-1: With this style the skis are V'd out, and you double-pole off one side only, skating back to that power-generating side. One of the clearest suggestions about how to V-skate comes from Dick Taylor. "Think of skating as double poling *over* one ski." You can already do it in the tracks over two skis. Try it again, noticing how your shoulders are square to the skis. Now, while stationary on smooth, untracked snow, splay your skis out in a V. Try planting your poles as if to double-pole over your right ski, squaring up your shoulders as you do. Yes, there is a problem: due to your squared shoulders, the left pole is between your legs. Not good for forward progress. So displace or stagger it, outside your left leg. That's why skating has that off-centered, high-handed look of the seasoned subway strap hanger. From that position, you'll curl forward in a familiar double pole. Although the right arm and pole are in position to supply more power than the left, make the motion simultaneous—keep the *double* in the double pole. As your poling concludes, you skate or step back over to the left ski.

You can walk through it like you're doing a herringbone on the flat. Ski and poles hit the snow together, then you step back and *forward*. Step? Better make that skate. You'll be pushing off an edged ski; it's the skater's equivalent of grip wax or gripping pattern. As the right ski comes onto the snow, it will be

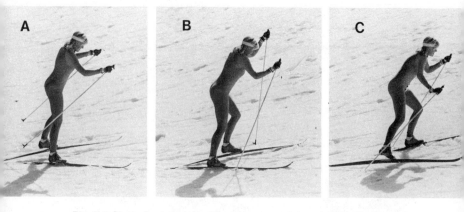

The V-1 Skate, from the side. The skier steps forward (D-E). Then by extending fully off the left ski (note heel, E), brings hips up over gliding ski (F). Again, note the similarities between the skater (D) and the strider (see

The V-1 Skate, from the rear. As with pure double poling, much of skating's power comes from "falling" onto your poles. Note the commitment in A with the feet close together. This skier is throwing a solid unit—shoulder and hip—into the skate. It is the Breaking Down the Door effect. The right

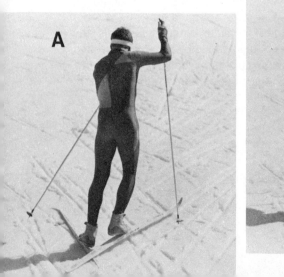

page 26, left photo): Both are preparing to launch themselves forward onto a gliding ski; their hips are "up" or "high" for greatest propulsion.

pole is the recipient of such effort, and in B props him up. A sure sign that the skier is twisted and poling over the right ski is the "hidden" left hand. The head leads the way back onto the left or recovery ski (C and D). It is a strong move with the whole body. Charge!

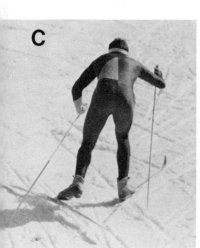

flat. As you skate, it will be edged progressively. To get a feel for edging and skating, abandon your poles and skate on skis alone. This will better accustom you to a complete weight shift from one ski to the other, to riding a single ski at a time for maximum glide, and to feeling the power that must come from the legs. Another way, and one that develops quick feet along with edging, is to skate through a figure eight slalom-style or skate out a big circle.

To get yourself lined up over one ski and then over the other is to use your head. Look to the "power" ski (the one you're poling over), then look to the "recovery" ski (the other one); feel your hips come up and over each ski. So, you're powering to the right, recovering or skating back to begin the cycle again.

In beginning skaters we notice a common problem. Many have the back and forth sequence right. But from the rear, they look like they're embracing an oversize partner. You can see both their hands, which suggests that they aren't twisting or poling over one ski and thus never fully committing to it. They're stuck in the middle between two skis, doing what one observer calls "the dancing bear." The dancing bear checks speed on the flats and nearly brings the skier to a halt on hills. If you're so afflicted—have a friend watch from behind—throw a

Unlike the skier in the middle, the one on the right isn't hiding her left hand. The result will be the incomplete weight transfer and compromised power of the leftmost skier, who's doing a version of the Dancing Bear.

bit of a left cross with the low hand (assuming you're powering to the right). You'll feel it pull you off of your left ski and put you properly onto the right one.

An ancillary problem here comes from trying to pole with too-straight arms. That high hand and power arm are in a position to supply little force. The remedy? *Answer the phone* (the Better Skating Bureau is on the line). Snug your high hand up a little closer to your ear.

Marathon skate: When we first saw marathon skating, it looked as if the skier was scootering himself along with one ski remaining in the track and bearing the skier's weight. To skate this way would be difficult for one kilometer, let alone a marathon. The marathon skate is another weight shift proposition. It's useful when the tracks are fast (after all, you're only tacking with one ski), and it's also a good tool for learning some of skating's essential moves.

Marathon skating has the same rhythm as the V-1 and a similar poling motion, but instead of recovering onto a splayed ski, you shift back onto the ski that is in the track. If you are hav-

The Marathon Skate involves the same commitment of weight as the V-1 (A). Lifting the heel of the ski still in the track will prompt a proper weight shift (B). The head still leads the skier back onto the recovery ski (C).

Flying on the flats with the V-2. Here, the poles hit the snow first (B) with the shoulders nearly square as in a double pole. The hips come up and over the gliding right ski (C-E), and the left foot is retrieved and brought in

ing a hard time committing to the skating ski—rocking out over it then back—try lifting the heel of the foot in the track, or even lifting the whole foot slightly. The marathon skate also can help you develop proper retrieval of the foot. Your feet must be together, under you, to get your hips up over the ski and put you in position to skate powerfully. Good skaters look like they're swaying back and forth over a fixed point, as if ballasted. Feel the difference between jumping to the side with your feet already straddled, and jumping with your feet together. With feet together, you get greater distance. In the marathon skate, you

Call it what you will (The Gunde or Open Field Skate), The Alternate V-2 is a relaxing way to speed over easier terrain. As in the V-2, the skier begins a double pole before coming down onto the gliding ski (A). Leading with the

close (F) for a more powerful skate off. Notice how much of a double pole has occurred before the skier skates onto the left ski (G).

can touch ankles for better retrieval.

The faster the conditions, the farther in front you should start the skating foot. Otherwise, by the time you've fully extended it, your hips will be so far back that you'll have to haul them back over to the ski in the track as you prepare for another skate.

Skiers who have trouble with the V-1 may find that doing what is in effect half of it—the marathon skate—is easier. If tracks run out as you marathon skate, you'll slide naturally into a V-1.

The V-2: The V-2 will put you on the fly on fast snow and

hands (E), the skier only skates or recovers back to the left instead of both skating and poling quickly, as in a V-2. (Compare D-F above.)

the flats. But it demands good balance and rhythm. Instead of the seamless slicing of the V-1, the V-2 has a catch-and-swing feel. That's because you start poling before you start skating. With poles hitting the snow before the gliding ski, you lose the stable tripod effect of the V-1. But since the skis are closer together at the beginning of the poling, your poles need not be staggered as much as in the V-1 to clear the skis. Thus your arms are more equal partners in poling. Start poling, then launch yourself out on a flat gliding ski. Swing your arms through to bring yourself up over your ski; it's all balance here, with no support from the poles. The gliding phase makes the V-2 less suitable for hills; there's just too much time in which to slow down.

Many of you downhill skiers probably have been V-2ing into lifts for much of your alpine career. But because of the short poles, you may have developed a habit of positioning the poles well behind you and palming them to squeeze out some extra thrust. Don't compromise the advantage of the longer poles by planting them as if they were short. Cure this by doing some straight double poling every so often while you're working on skating.

Alternate V-2: For downhill skiers the alternate V-2 is a way station on the road to the V-1. For everyone, it's an easy way to cover ground on the flat. It's easy because it combines the syncopation of pole and ski from the V-2 with the legs-only recovery skate of the V-1. If you're having trouble synchronizing the glide leg and the poles here or in the V-2, try the following. Imagine there is a string attaching your hands to the knee of your glide leg and ski. As your hands come up to begin the double pole, they bring the glide leg up with them. When the poles hit the snow, they cut the cord as it were, and you skate out onto the glide ski. Poles hit first, then ski.

Diagonal or herringbone skate: Seeing the diagonal skate from the side, you might mistake it for a diagonal stride. It almost is. The arms work one at a time, just as in the herringbone. But as you flare the ski out, make it slide as it hits the snow. There's plenty of sashay in this skate—or there should be to keep the skis sliding. This is the lowest skating gear for uphills, the easiest and least taxing way up—the skate of last resort.

Jump skating: Jump skating is basically a V-1 skate with a pronounced bound from one ski to the other. Use it over the

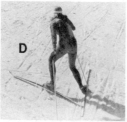

Everyman's Elevator. This is the easiest way uphill—as useful for the elite as for the inexperienced. Years ago we called this the Flying Herringbone. It's a herringbone rhythm with added slide. The hand and foot work is the same as in the diagonal stride. Alternate hand and foot forward (B). When you look over the weighted ski, hips follow, and the skis keep sliding, rather than slowing to a less effective stop-and-start movement.

Jump Skate is skating at its most ballistic. The skier just doesn't step up, as in a V-1, but launches himself. Note the heels: To get this airborne, the skier must bound off the left leg.

tops of short hills or anywhere you want to accelerate. It's quite taxing, however. As we write, it's still not clear whether the jump skate will catch on.

Free skating: Call it what you will. Free skating relies primarily on the legs, and you move like a speed skater. Squeeze out even more speed by swinging your arms. Swinging the arms helps you accelerate on downhills. But consider whether you should skate or maintain a tuck to rest arms and legs and bring your pulse down. Still, some free skating from an upright position will really help your sense of edging and of the skating power of coiling and uncoiling legs.

Situational Skating

Skating soft: When the snow comes up soft, whether due to a dump of fresh powder that resists packing down or ice that is machine-chewed into the consistency of sand, a skater's waltz can turn into a skater's slog. Try a longer ski for better flotation in the fluff—skis normally used for diagonal striding should work fine—and make some alterations in the technique. If you weight your skis a little too much on the inside or the outside, the snow can cave in on you. If you try to power through, there's a good chance you'll be engulfed. Since you can't sit on your skis as long in this kind of snow, try to be quicker and lighter.

Skating slithery: When the snow is crumpled and crusty or greasy enough to throw you around like the ruts on a muddy road, it's hard to ride a ski for very long and still stay in balance. Where we ski, it's sometimes called "stagger snow." In these conditions, the tripodlike stability of the V-1—along with a quicker tempo—is helpful.

Skating steep: Skaters now slide up hills as if the laws of gravity had been repealed. If you're new to skating, remember that with a little more time on skis, what first appeared to be headwalls will begin to feel decidedly flat. At the very worst you can always herringbone; chances are, though, that even here you can get the skis sliding into a herringbone skate. But if you

Having trouble getting a feel for edging? Can't manage a full weight shift? Here's the cure. In free skating, the swing's the thing, and hands lead the way. Head and hips follow; even without poles, this skate's no different in principle from the others.

want to maintain a faster V-1, you'll have to make a few modifications.

We've talked to some top coaches about hills. Canadian Ski Team coach Marty Hall has an overview. Everything is related to gliding, as he sees it. On steeper hills, you simply don't glide as much. Your range of motion is shorter; the slower you go, the lower you go. Former U.S. Ski Team coach Mike Gallagher calls the movement of the upper body "trunk stroke." When skating uphill, it's shorter. There's less time to work the arms *and* the upper body before you lose the glide. Our neighbor, Shamus Daly, a coaching genius with juniors, favors a quick compression with the upper body, making sure that you look from one ski to the other to get a good weight transfer. That will help you keep the ski sliding. You'll lose momentum quickly if you first put the ski down and *then* shift weight over

On steep hills, there's no time for the full up and down of a complete double pole with the skate. The body works in a more limited mid-range. Most important is stepping up the hill (B-C), then getting hips up and over that leading ski.

and try to make it slide.

Beyond that, treat the hill like a snowy staircase, stepping up it. This will be harder to do if you haven't compressed quickly, as soon as the pole goes in the snow and hips have fallen back. To feel how vital it is to ski with high hips, try sitting back, dropping onto an imaginary chair, and stepping forward. Contrast that Chuck Berry position with the ease of stepping forward once the hips are up. If you're having trouble with a hill, Daly suggests taking it in segments, skiing what you can in good style until you are able to take it all in a gulp.

Skiing sidehill: Often a skating trail will be higher on one side than another, known as sidehill. Although you can still get an argument, most skaters will double-pole onto the *uphill* ski, skating back with aid of gravity. Same thing on curves: double-pole onto the *inside* ski.

CHAPTER 5

Downhill

When you listen to the stories of free-heeled heroism circulating in local touring centers at the end of the day, what you hear isn't flat, or of the flat. It's boasting the downhill with a decidedly Newtonian bent. "I shot the chute," "I made an impossible corner," "I flew like the Royal Ballet," "I cartwheeled forever."

Flats are a test of fitness; downhills are a test of boldness. The "let's work" side of cross-country is easy on your joints and good for aging bodies. But we're not going to be parochial about this. Most relish the "less work" side of cross-country, which is going downhill fast, slow, headfirst, tailfirst, and even sideways. Downhill is just plain fun.

It's fun and different than anything else we do because it's free speed and you can let go. The friction of skis against the snow does 90 percent of the work. As alpine instructing virtuoso Lito Tejada-Flores says, "The skier becomes a superman or superwoman moving through space with an ease never found in everyday life.... An excited beginner can fly down those small practice hills faster than Olympic track-and-field champions could run down them."

Forget the alleged conspiracy between gravity and well-waxed skis: if you point the skis downhill, they seem to have a mind of their own. Let's talk about a confederacy between skis and gravity. A positive attitude can unite skis and gravity and have a calming effect as you approach altitude. Many people arrive at local touring centers and ask, "Where are the easy trails?" These accomplished gliders, skaters, and uphill gradient gulpers all start listing the old "can't-cope-with-down-slope"

Three-pinning in Canada's Bugaboos

Embrace the downhills.

epitaphs for skinny skis—no edges, no heel hold-down, no ankle support, no control, no way I can get down. But don't listen. Don't look at downhill as a problem or an enemy.

Incline is everything in skiing. Although, as a cross-country skier, you (unlike downhillers) can slide without it and even climb up it. If you don't want hills, OK, but there is excitement to be had. Speeding securely down hills is rather addictive and a real tonic for skiers whose local touring trails are getting too familiar. For beginning cross-country skiers, the downhill sections, not the flats, are the real challenge to overcome on the way to overall enjoyment of the sport.

Downhill skiers are adding cross-country to their winter pleasures and cross-country skiers are riding the lifts with loose heels and heading for steep backcountry terrain on light equipment. Many slopes traditionally skied with heavy ski-mountaineering equipment are now being skied with three-pin equipment. Cross-country downhill on metal-edged skis has even become a sport unto itself, a new challenge, a new use of nordic gear. It is three times the fun of alpine skiing at half the speed.

All over the country skiers seem to be rediscovering the early days of alpine skiing of the 1930s. Cross-country skiers in the town we live in often head to the top of Mount Mansfield, Vermont's highest peak, to ski the Teardrop and the Bruce, magnificent if narrow alpine trails cut in 1937 and since abandoned. They are available now to skiers willing to climb up in order to ski down—whatever their equipment. Not only are we using some of the old trails, but by looking at photographs of skiers in the 1930s—their low, stable stance utilizing extreme edging—we get a good image of the technique a cross-country skier needs for skiing down hills.

Remember that even good alpine skiers were beginners once. A nordic skier may even have an advantage in learning downhill. The Professional Ski Instructors of America suggest that first-time alpine skiers start with nordic. Why? It's easier to move around and sense balance on light skis. The light equipment responds to the most minute shifts in incline. No inch of terrain is wasted.

Sure, it's an inescapable fact that the all-terrain design of cross-country equipment, which allows you to go uphill, compromises downhill control. But the compromise is not as much as doomsayers would have you believe. In fact, today's equipment gives far more control than that of a decade ago. It's a surprise and a delight how much you can do on cross-country gear. Plus, at today's modern touring centers, the trails are wider and the grooming far more sophisticated. Often, the terrain will turn your skis for you.

Fresh powder on the Teardrop Trail, Mt. Mansfield, Vermont

So how can you enjoy cross-country downhill? There's little problem if you're athletic or a good alpine skier. But what if you're neither? The answer is technique. You can learn enough technique to get down most hills if you stick to basics: traversing and sideslipping, wedges and hockey stops. "If I swing my skis sideways, and push with my heels, they turn!" says eighty-year-old John Dostal (senior), after skiing solo from the heights of the Trapp trail system.

Not to be outdone, Gillette's seventy-five-year-old mother, rock steady and sure after half a century of skiing, stays within her comfort zone. Done so for years. She simply snowplows (wedges) down every incline, cruise control activated, pulse at resting beat.

Body Position

Ski downhill in the ready but relaxed position you would use to receive a tennis serve, with your weight centered over both feet. Bend your ankles and press forward against the top lace of your boots. This causes your knees to flex forward as well. Flexed knees act as shock absorbers and make steering

Keep glasses clear, socks matched, knees bent, and hands low and in front.

At slow speeds, relax on your skis, with knees bent.

possible. As German-born instructor, Adi Yoerg, says, "You cannot ski with knees like the goat."

Though you flex your knees, you'll find that, with hands up in the air (victim of an alpine hold-up?), you'll be hard-pressed to make a turn or to be secure even on a straight downhill run. Your body follows your hands. Keep hands low and spread in front as if you're gripping bicycle handlebars. Hands that are too high or too far back (that is, out of your field of vision) throw you off balance. Gymnasts on a balance beam use their arms for positioning in the same way.

Straight Run

Letting your skis run straight down the fall line of a gentle, packed slope to a natural stop is a good way to get used to a bit of speed. Keep your skis hip-width apart for side-to-side stability and your poles angled backward to avoid catching the stray bush or skier. This, by the way, is not just an exercise for the rankest beginner but something to return to often as you find downhill slopes on which you can simply let your skis run. In some snow conditions it is more secure to run straight with more speed than you might like than to try to pull out by turning.

Aerodynamic nose-warming posture, aka tucking

Later on as you begin skiing trails, try getting all you can out of each straight downhill. You'll be amazed how much speed you can carry onto the flats. This is all free distance covered, normal breathing restored. Try tucking (crouching) for more speed. If your legs are fatigued, rest by keeping your legs straighter and lean over in your upper body only.

When trails roll and dip, you'll find that, not only do you have to maintain balance side to side, but also fore and aft. To do this on rolling terrain, drop into a telemark position by pushing one flexed knee ahead of the other, as if you are genuflecting. It's the best way to absorb bumps and hollows.

Getting Up After

If your repertoire of stopping techniques is minimal, and you're on the verge of blowing it on a downhill run, don't hesitate to sit down—put bottom to snow and slide on your seat to a stop. We've seen plenty of experts extricate themselves from a heady schuss by plopping down to avoid an eggbeater. Because the equipment is lightweight, cross-country falls are pretty safe, but you may have to do some disentangling once stopped. And, unless you're endowed with Neanderthal arms, you need a bit of technique to hoist yourself upright without getting uptight in the battle with gravity.

To get up, roll on your side, then onto both knees and stand up.

To get up from a fall, roll over onto your side so your skis are parallel, downhill from you and across the fall line of the slope so they will not slide forward or back. If you are submerged in deep snow, form an X with your poles to provide a stable platform from which to push off. Then simply move forward onto your knees, rock back onto your feet, and stand up. No thrashing necessary.

Step Turns

The most obvious way to turn on cross-country skis is simply to pick one up, point it in the direction you want to go, and bring the other one over next to it. It's called a step turn. It will feel a lot less awkward if you try to pick up and turn the tip of the ski rather than the whole ski. At first you'll feel somewhat defensive, barely able to get the skis around in time. Soon you'll be scampering, stepping quickly into or out of the tracks and around looming trees. You can get more aggressive and indulge in accelerating skating turns, pushing off with each skate. This is familiar to alpine skiers and to skaters on blades.

Stepping and skating are often the only turns you can do when you are locked into deep-set machine tracks or dealing

On step turns, let your hands lead you around.

with untracked, tricky snow that catches tails and edges of skis. Little speed is lost. A single skate turn will accomplish a minimal change of direction; several skates in succession will cover a larger radius. To stop, do a series of steps until you're headed somewhat back up the hill. Use skate turns to negotiate corners on the flat when your speed is fairly fast, and on downhills when your speed is not so fast that you must make a parallel carved turn.

To make a skate turn, keep your knees flexed and hands low for balance. Edge your outside ski for a secure platform from which to step. The critical ingredient is the weight shift from the outside ski to the inside ski. It's similar to the weight shift forward in the diagonal stride, but here also to the side, almost duck-footed. What you're after is a definite step from one ski to the other. Most errors in making a good skate turn come from being caught in between with weight on both skis. It should be one smooth movement.

Whether you realize it or not (disregarding style points), you can now get down most hills by combining traverses (straight runs across a hill), step turns, and kick turns. You don't even have to know how to turn on the move. Here's how you do it. First slide across the hill in a slow traverse with your ski tips barely pointing downhill. Keep most of your weight on your downhill ski. If the slope steepens, advance your uphill ski. Then stop by stepping laterally up into the hill. Once stationary, turn by doing a kick turn. In this way you can zigzag down most any hill.

Shift weight to step around.

In a wide wedge you're plowing snow. Tracks will tell if you're leaving the proper wide wake.

Wedging

Stopping or turning on your cross-country skis will be a lot easier if you've made the acquaintance of your edges.

Stand stationary across the hill. Roll your ankles into the slope to edge your skis. Try to push your downhill ski outward (downward). It won't move if it is edged. Now flatten your downhill ski on the snow and push it outward. It will skid easily (sideslip).

Newly sensitive to the edging of the skis, you're ready to develop some resources for stopping, unless you prefer your descents quick and free of control. The place to begin is with a wedge.

Pick a packed, easy slope. Let your skis run straight downhill, keeping your knees flexed and hands forward and apart. Ready for the wedge? Weight your heels. Spread the tails of your skis apart equally by sinking into a wedge position and gliding along. Twist your heels apart. Keep your skis fairly flat and the tips together. It feels like the skis are brushing or plowing over the snow.

Ready to stop? Roll your ankles inward to set the skis on their inside edges and dig in to brake. If skis are over-edged they may cross; if they are too flat they will not brake. The wider the wedge and the more you edge by bearing down, the slower you'll go. Keep the pressure on and you'll come to a gradual stop, not on the proverbial dime but on a string of dimes. (One thing we've found is that the wedge is oversold as a means to put the brakes on firmly on any but the easiest downhills. To brake on a steep hill you'll have to turn up into the hill—but more on that later.)

The wider apart you hold your knees, the more effective your snowplow. Knock-knees aren't effective: bend your knees forward, not together, and keep them far enough apart to hold a beachball between them.

A moving half wedge is a good way to feel edging. Traverse a groomed slope at an easy angle. With much of your weight on your uphill ski, push your downhill ski out into a half plow. Edge the ski to the inside to slow your speed and stop.

Here's another way to initiate a wedge stop. Head straight down a gentle slope with your skis parallel. Before gaining much speed, sink and spread into a definite wedge. But don't stop completely. Just before you lose momentum, draw your skis back parallel, gain speed, wedge again, parallel, wedge, and so on. Try this long enough to allow a sequence of several near-stops.

A half wedge is the easiest way to get a feel for edging. It is also the best way to slow down in tracks; most of the skier's weight is over the ski in the track. He's easing onto the wedging ski to slow down.

Many people produce only a lopsided chicken wing wedge. Look at your tracks in the snow: both skis should be skidding, leaving a wake rather than a line. If not, correct by bringing *both* hips square to the direction you are heading so that your skis are equally weighted. Letting one hip fall back straightens that knee, makes you crooked on your skis, and leaves you with only a half-effective braking force. Arms are often the culprit here. Skiers pull elbows up and out in an imitation wedge, hoping that the legs will, somehow, follow. Keeping your hands square and in front is a good device for squaring your hips.

Wedge Turn

The wedge turn is the turn of first resort, easily initiated by putting more pressure on one ski. It is extremely stable, the foundation for more advanced turns, and it teaches the skill of steering.

Head downhill in your regular gliding wedge. As you press your skis out, shift your weight and stand on the outside ski that is pointed in the direction you want to go. Lean to the outside of the turn as if centrifugal force were throwing you to the outside. Apply heel pressure and edge the ski against the snow so it will hold. Steer around with your knees by twisting your knee and foot the way you want to go. Lean right to turn left, like pushing a tiller away from you in a boat.

It's not uncommon to see a skier hurtling downhill while protesting loudly that the skis won't turn. Usually, it's caused by

Wedge Turns: From your stable hands-forward, knees-flexed position (A), put pressure on and edge your outside ski, then steer your knees and feet in the same direction (B).

just a couple of errors. The skier may have put his skis on edge before getting into a snowplow. Sliding downhill on parallel rails makes it virtually impossible to come around. Remember, it's a wedge turn. Think (and get into) a wedge, then apply pressure to turn.

But keeping proper pressure on the ski is hard for those who lean into the turn. It's as if they believe that getting the brain over to the right means that the body will somehow follow. But it won't, because pressure has been taken off the downhill ski: they've shifted the wrong way.

Another common error is mistaking your body for your skis: that is, struggling to throw your heavy upper body around the corner. Remember your skis are designed to turn. Let them do the work. We actually like to see novices emphasize leaning away from the turn to shift maximum weight onto the outside, turning ski so it becomes dominant and can perform.

If you're having trouble with the turn, put your hands on your bent knees. (This also puts you in the proper body position.) When you want to turn, simply press in on your outside or downhill knee with your hand. Push left knee in to go right, push right knee in to go left. Feel the rhythm. Pushing on the downhill knee helps turning in three critical ways: (1) steers the downhill knee in the direction you want to turn; (2) places your weight on the downhill ski; (3) edges your downhill ski so it will carve around.

Or try this. If you want to make a right turn, imagine you're carrying a heavy suitcase (in our haunts a full sap bucket) in your left hand. Let the weight pull your shoulder and arm down, putting pressure on your left ski—pressure that will make a turn.

Lots of pressure on your downhill ski can make you stop. You can make a wedge turn that will really stop you on a dime in case you're hurtling downhill and come upon a skier fallen in front of you. Make a very sharp, emphatic wedge turn up into the side of the trail and step the uphill ski over next to the downhill steering ski with a motion like your old high school two-step dance. This is really a natural finish to a snowplow turn and is the gateway to parallel skiing, giving you a feeling of completing turns with maximum control. After all, your uphill ski isn't doing much in the turn—stepping emphatically off it will swing you around faster. Being able to stand on one leg, even momentarily, is great progress.

Sideslipping: Driving ankles and knees into the slope puts skis on edge. Roll ankles down to flatten them out and sideslip.

Feeling good? Ski a little faster and stretch your turns out into longer arcs. How do you add speed? By bringing the tails of your skis closer together in a smaller wedge. What happens in this fast, narrow wedge? The edges bite less. Almost in spite of yourself, you discover that you are drifting sideways at the end of each turn. The skis feel like they've broken loose in comparison to the old edge-grinding wedge. You can feel that a flatter ski offers less resistance to turning. This accidental skidding traverse across the hill is the foundation of the next level of turns called christies.

At this point you have enough downhill techniques to handle a lot of hills. Practice some, but go out and get some mileage under your skis. Ski, ski, and ski. Skiing for a week straight will do more for your progress than a season of weekend skiing.

Edge Sense

Before trying advanced christie turns, you've got to get a handle on a third basic skill. You've learned lateral stepping and wedge steering. Now you need edge control. There are infinite gradations of tilting a ski depending how much you want to schuss or brake. The best way to come to an understanding with your edges is by sideslipping down an incline. To do it well, you have to do everything that is involved in parallel turns, except the actual turning.

Stand across a groomed slope. To cling to the slope without slipping, you naturally roll your ankles and knees into the slope. The edges bite into the snow. Now relax your lower legs so that your skis flatten, and you slip sideways down the hill. To stop yourself edge the skis again. Try a long sideslip and vary your speed by adjusting your edges. Or try a zigzag series of sideslips diagonally forward and backward by shifting your weight.

You ski with your feet. Sideslipping increases your awareness of your feet and hones the pressure and feeling for the snow that you get through them. It encourages you to keep your weight on the downhill ski. To compensate for your knees twisted into the slope, lean out from the slope with your upper body so that, overall, your weight is directly over your skis. This body bending is called angulation.

Sideslipping is also useful as a technique; hills too steep, too rocky, or too nasty can always be sideslipped.

Easy Christies

A christie is a turn in which your skis end up parallel. The christie is a faster, more definite, and prettier turn than a wedge.

It's easy to start from what you already know: a super-stable wedge with hands forward and knees flexed (A). To get ready to turn, shift your weight to the outside (left) ski so it will skid, and lift your inside (right) pole (B). Plant your inside pole, lift your inside ski (C), and step it in parallel. Now continue skidding around. You've ended in a parallel turn. Notice your body position is the same hands-forward, knees-flexed position as when you started, except your skis are parallel.

Stem Christie: Start by sliding across the slope like you've done before. Keep your weight mostly on your downhill ski (A). Pick up and step out your uphill ski (B) into your familiar wedge. That ski is now pointing in the direction you want to turn (C). Plant your inside pole and shift all your weight onto the outside ski. Now it's easy to pick up the inside ski (D), lay it in parallel and skid around the turn in your stable hands-forward, knees-flexed position (E).

78

It moves you toward a parallel while maintaining the security of a wedge. It's a good braking maneuver, because you can jam the tails of your skis into the snow. There are two easy christies that work from skills you've already learned: the sideslip christie and the stem christie.

To begin the sideslip christie, start out in your familiar wedge, then come around the corner and almost complete the turn in a wedge. Your weight is on your outside steering ski, which is already turning and skidding over the snow. Now simply lift the inside ski up and slide or step it in parallel to the steering ski. Flex your knees and ankles as you set the ski down. Keep your stance wide for balance. Now that your skis are parallel, they both will skid sideways, just as in the sideslipping routine.

For your first christie turns, wedge through the fall line, then close your skis, bringing them parallel. Your wedge will get narrower as you get better. Gradually reduce the snowplow part of the turn as your balance improves, and start the skidding action sooner. Now you're bringing your skis parallel earlier and moving toward parallel skiing, leaving behind the wedge.

The stem christie is a little more advanced, but it's still easy. It introduces you to the parallel part of the turn earlier. Begin by traversing a slope, skis parallel and weight on the downhill ski. Step or push the uphill ski out into a wedge. This is easy, because all the while you're secure on your downhill ski. You've pointed the ski more in the direction of the turn, changing its edge. Shift your weight onto it. Now you can effortlessly pull your other ski in parallel and skid around the turn. In this position, traverse the hill parallel in preparation for the next turn. By bringing your skis parallel at the end of the turn, you learn to pick up one ski and float it so that you're not always on both skis as you are in the wedge.

You've just made a big transition, from always standing on both skis like a beginner to shifting from one ski to the other. Remember the old wedge turn? The outside ski did the work; the inside ski seemed pointed in the opposite direction, contrary to the new direction. What if the inside ski were floating along in the same direction? Wouldn't things be easier? Standing on the dominant, steering ski is the key to advanced skiing. Some call it one-legged skiing.

We're not asking you to balance on one leg *ad infinitum* to the bottom of the mountain. We're asking you to do some-

On radical terrain, recovery is everything.

thing you do every day: shift your weight from one foot to the other like a steered, slow-action walk or run. Or a diagonal cross-country stride. Or a step turn. The motor skills are already there. The easiest way to draw on them for downhill skiing is to traverse across a gentle hill and balance only on your downhill ski. Stop and go back the other way on the other leg.

It's worth trying, because as you start into advanced turns, you'll already be in on the best-kept secret in skiing: putting all your weight on your outside ski gives you the most turning power for your money. You've freed yourself to slide the inside ski in so it drifts alongside, parallel.

Hockey Stop

Let's leave the ABCs of technique behind for a minute, and try something that will give the sensation of turning both skis at the same time: the hockey stop. You begin by skiing straight downhill in a wide-track schuss, crouching lower than normal. Violently twist both skis sideways and screech to a

In uniform or out, the hockey stop demands that skis swivel but everything else stays headed downhill.

stop, like a hockey skater stopping on a dime. Force your skis to bite into the snow. The hockey stop also works as an emergency halt if someone skis in front of you unexpectedly, or if you discover a stream cutting across your path during late spring skiing.

Parallel Turns

You don't necessarily have to do parallel turns to be a competent skier on cross-country skis. But if you're comfortable with stem christies, parallel turns are only a short slide away and will give you more control through a faster, tighter turn. Despite what you may have heard, you do not have to be an alpine skier to learn to ski parallel. We've often seen beginning skiers produce a parallel turn instead of the intended stem christie or, rarely, snowplow turns. However, let's fact it, the only skiers who can really crank parallel turns on skinny skis in all conditions are expert alpine skiers. So, although you can learn how to parallel on nordic skis as outlined here, if you want to get hot, spring for a few tickets at the nearest alpine ski area, rent alpine equipment, and schuss and swivel along with the alpiners.

To make any turn, whether it's a stem or a parallel, you have to steer one or both skis in a new direction, and you must change that ski's edge. The following parallel turn requires you to pivot or twist both skis with your knees and change both edges simultaneously. You have to do this at the start of the turn, not halfway through as with an easy christie.

With free-heeled equipment, you'll make it easier on yourself if you really bend your knees and ankles. Skiing parallel with a deep-knee and ankle bend can almost compensate for the power you miss by not being in stiff alpine boots. So get down, almost crouch, to lock your foot to your knee for maximum steering action.

Lean into each turn like a bicycle rider. Add some speed to help smooth things out. Do longer turns, stay in your wide stance, and emphasize your knee and ankle bend. If you feel wobbly on your free-heeled bindings, thrust your heels around to complete turns.

To do relaxed advanced parallels, you'll have to add anticipation. Anticipation means that your upper body turns downhill before your skis and legs; your torso "anticipates," or winds up, for the turn. An instant later your legs and skis unwind and pivot underneath, and the turn is complete. In other words, the body is preturned, and it ushers the skis into the turn.

Anticipation also helps good skiers link their turns in a fluid motion. As Tejada-Flores says, "Think of it as a total pattern of skiing in which legs and skis work actively against the heavy and relatively stable upper body, building a kind of tension at the end of one turn that can be 'released' into the start of a new turn. This is the single most important idea (or technique) in advanced alpine skiing."

There's more, however, to the parallel. To anchor your upper body just before the skis unwind, plant your downhill

Olympic downhiller Pete Patterson showing good anticipation on South American snow.

pole. Unweight your skis so you can turn them more easily. Usually this is done by rising up off your skis to take the pressure off them.

To get the feeling of how twisting at the waist will help to start each turn, mountain guide Allan Bard suggests standing stationary across the hill. Turn your upper body and look straight down the fall line. Put your pole in the snow. Now, pick up your downhill ski, transmitting the springlike twist in your waist to the ski, causing it to turn.

How do you learn? You can introduce yourself to all this via an uphill christie. Start in a traverse, sink into a sideslip by pushing the tails of both skis downhill, and steer your skis uphill, while keeping your upper body facing downhill. For a little help here, station a friend at the bottom of the slope and keep your eyes on him as you make your turns. When this feels good, add a pole plant as you stop. This locks your torso in place. You should feel wound up, ready to trigger the new turn. It's called a preturn.

Now you're ready to turn parallel. After your pole plant, rise up and forward to unweight the skis. The skis will flatten, start to unwind, and turn downhill on their own. Shift your weight onto the uphill ski and commit yourself to it, leaning on it as it becomes the downhill ski. You're around. As you begin to link your turns, the preturn you learned in the uphill christie exercise is supplied by the end of the preceding turn. The end of one turn starts the next. Everything evolves into a smooth series.

Linking Turns

Turns downhill are actually easier when more than one is done, so that the ending of one turn sets you up for the next, establishing a rhythm and cadence that blends the individual ingredients of turning into one flowing motion—it's called linking your turns. Once you learn the ABCs of doing a snowplow, skate, stem christie, parallel, or telemark turn, try to link several together. This is what skiing is really about: negotiating the slope as if all your turns were tied to each other. "She can really crank her skis right and left" is truly a complimentary way of saying someone is a good skier.

The snowplow shortswing: This exercise is a great way to feel the rhythm of linked turns and steering power. It forces

The writing's on the wall.

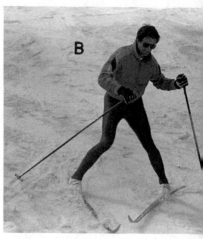

Snowplow Shortswing: Sashaying down the slope in linked power steering wedges (A) gives you a feeling that the finish of one turn sets you up for the start of the next (B).

you to flex your knees and ankles to steer your skis. If you can do this, we guarantee you can do advanced turns.

Head straight down a gentle slope in a *shallow* wedge, and do quick and continuously linked turns. As soon as your weight comes onto one ski and you start to turn, get off that ski and onto the other and turn in that direction. Think of it as making decisive half turns, almost bouncing from side to side, turn to turn.

Linked parallel turns: Work from a platform to set up for the turn. Check your speed by setting the edges. Push your heels down into the snow and flex your knees and ankles forward and angle them sideways into the hill. At the same time plant your downhill pole and punch your hand forward, over the pole. Sink with your knees and plant your pole to trigger the turn.

To keep your weight on your downhill ski, lean out and over it—that is, away from and not into the hill, even while your knees are driving into the hill. In this way you avoid banking your turns like a water-skier—a habit that usually leads to falls on cross-country skis.

Unweight to release your edges by springing up and forward to get your weight off both skis. This frees them so they will run to the fall line. It's like pushing in the clutch on an automobile. Once the friction is released, you can shift gears. (In skiing, you're after a shift of the edges.)

Now press down and forward to steer around. The harder

Parallel turns: Start in your stable hands-forward, knees-flexed position with your skis parallel but comfortably apart (A). Trigger the turn by pressing down with your knees and heels to set your edges, and "anchoring" your upper body by planting your inside pole. Keep your upper body facing down the hill to "anticipate" or wind up for the coming turn (B). Rise up to unweight your skis so they will pivot. Let your legs unwind under your upper body (C). Angle your skis to the inside so the edges will bite (D). Press your knees down and forward to steer around. Drive your outside hand forward also (E). The finish of your turn sets you up for starting the next one (F).

the pressure, the sharper the turn. Change your ski edges as you come through the turn. Push down with your heels and drive your outside hand in the direction of the turn. Bend your knees, especially the outside one, for maximum steering and edging. Weight the downhill ski.

Get set for the next turn by checking your momentum with a preturn. Press the edges of both skis against the snow and face your shoulders downhill. The end of one turn becomes the start of the next.

Poling

At this point in the anatomy lesson you should start thinking about your hands and poles. Your skis will do the work if your hands are in the right place. Good alpine poling is like a secret weapon. The hands really begin the turn. You are essentially turning around your downhill pole. Planting it decisively is a way of saying "get ready" to turn your skis. Reaching out with your hand keeps your body centered and over your skis, ready as you initiate the turn. Planting the pole makes you solid to begin the turn. It serves as a steadying point. Keep driving that downhill hand forward throughout the turn, or you will ski past your pole, twisting your body back and out of position and reducing the bite of your edges on the snow. If you're having a hard time getting from one turn to the other, check your hands. A decisive yet smooth pole plant sets your rhythm.

While your downhill hand is planting the pole, what is your other hand doing? If it is lazy and has drifted back past

Planting the pole triggers the turn.

your hip, it will be hard to bring the skis around for your next turn. No matter which hand is planting the pole, they should both be out to the side and in front (within your field of vision), as if you were embracing an enormous snowman or holding the handlebars of a grossly oversized bicycle, so that you'll be square on your skis for easier and quicker turns. The outward motion of the outside hand has a miraculous effect of gaining more ski edge and thus falling down less.

For those who have had the distinction of learning to ski downhill after years of cross-country, there is a functional difference in using long cross-country poles for doing alpine-style turns. The shorter alpine poles, planted vertically, bring you forward onto your skis. Planting a cross-country pole vertically will put your hand so high that your weight will be thrown back off your skis. If you are doing only lift-served skiing on your sticks, use a shorter pole (but don't expect as much out of your diagonal stride or double poling as you're heading for the lift). When using a normal-length cross-country pole, you must recreate the short pole feeling. You'll probably find that you have to cock your wrist, getting the hand forward and the basket way out in front of the pole plant. You can also choke up on

From this position, driving the left hand will bring you around right.

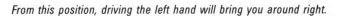

your long poles (as with a baseball bat). The new, well-balanced adjustable poles allow the renaissance skier to do it all—up, down, and level—with one set of sticks.

Speeding without Spilling

Even the most competent ski swivelers get into situations where turns will not be the order of the day. The time will come when you simply have to ride it out. High speeds don't necessarily have to be terrifying (indeed they may become addictive).

If you want to hang on in high-speed bombing, hold your hands low and in front to keep your position low. Flex your ankles and knees to steer and to absorb shock. Keep your feet apart for stability. It's as if you're rising up slightly out of the downhill racer's tuck, extending your hands forward and to the side. If you're hurtling through a sweeping corner, stay in this position and steer with your hands, driving the outside hand in the direction of the turn. At high speeds this will pull you around a turn as long as you stay low.

Spilling

In pursuit of downhill competence, falling is inevitable. While it is much more likely to happen in the hills, it can, of course, occur on the flats: consider the ski-stopping shred of birchbark in the tracks. Or the infrequently seen errant pole plant that puts the basket solidly over the tip of a ski, an entanglement from which recovery is virtually impossible.

Face it; as skiers we've all fallen and will fall again. With little choice in the matter, let us relax and not let it get in the way of our continuing efforts to be better or go faster on our skis. Looked at as failure, falling will only make you miserable. We've all seen the skier who wipes out and, embarrassed by the abrupt intersection of rear and snow, jumps instantly to his feet, quickly brushing off the snow, and takes a covert look around to see who might have witnessed. Or the beginning skier in a class who grimly mutters after a tumble, "That's the third one." But for the skier who's airborne, en route to the inevitable crater, who realizes that he's been indulging in, as Thomas McGuane puts it, "a bravura extension beyond his own abilities," the fall merely marks forward progress (emphasis on bravura).

Not only will falling become less onerous, it may become downright addictive. You'll relish the chance for display and pay more attention to style. No longer satisfied with a simple sit down, you'll hope for something more flamboyant. Going for more speed will allow for a Flying Buttocks Arrest ("Parallel Bun Stop," for more advanced skiers). If the density of the snowpack is right, a Thundering Buttocks Arrest can be achieved. Points may be awarded for flagrant travel over the tips of the skis, for securing maximum air time, for devastation of equipment, and for pruning and removal of shrubs and trees.

Worried about falling in front of others? Soon you'll long for an onlooker to substantiate claims made later for distance of air travel. Or for a witness to a windmilling, seemingly endless, high-speed gainer, through whom you can relive the flailing and burrowing. For you, for all of us, there will be that giddy moment when time seems to have stopped, when we're weightless, free, arcing over the tips of our skis, dead certain we're about to bury our heads.

A Word to Alpine Skiers

Skiing downhill on cross-country skis is good practice for alpine skiers. No longer can you "cheat" while turning and get away with it because of the stable holding power of alpine equipment. Downhill cross-country skiing will bring you back to basics. You'll learn a tremendous amount about balance, weight, steering, and edging which is directly applicable to alpine.

Relative to alpine equipment, cross-country gear is responsive on downhills. The skis are lighter, narrower, more flexible, and may or may not have metal edges; boots are much more flexible, and heels lift freely off the skis. This means less control and stability than available on alpine equipment.

But we've found that the problem is not so much equipment as misinformation and superstition. Don't assume that just because the equipment is different you have no control. One expert alpine skier in a cross-country class protested that she couldn't do parallel turns on cross-country skis. Had she ever tried? No, but she'd often been told that they couldn't be done. Her instructor urged her to give them a try. The result, not surprisingly, was a dozen short-swing parallel turns and ongoing bliss. Other alpine skiers may not have such immediate results, but they'll find they ski pretty much the same way on both kinds of equipment, with some subtle differences.

If you are a good alpine skier or racer, then everything you do in alpine has direct carry-over into cross-country downhill skiing. You are used to edging and unweighting in turns, keeping your hands low and in front, holding your upper body neutral, and getting the most out of your equipment. The strength to drive hard must be combined with flexibility. But if you are an intermediate or novice alpine skier and are used to turning by banking or swiveling, you will have to make some adjustments to be competent on skinny skis—nothing more than a little more edging and a little more unweighting.

Modern alpine equipment permits you to turn by banking (leaning your body into the hill), with less edging, more skidding, and less emphasis on the position of the hands. Metal edges are so sharp and boots so stiff that it is not necessary to edge radically for the ski to hold and carve a turn. Since your heel is firmly attached to the ski, you can press forward and down on the top of your ski to initiate the turn with the ski tip. Loose-heeled cross-country equipment, however, allows you to press *around* a turn, but not forward and down. Further, the tip of a light cross-country ski is flexible, so you do not carve a turn on it as with an alpine ski; you turn on the midbody of the ski.

Gillette flouting the 55-mph speed limit

First the pole plant, then the face plant

To compensate for the light equipment, your weight must be right over the center of your skis or you'll be on your rear end. It's not easy to balance on a narrow, sliding platform, especially when you are wearing what is essentially a soft running shoe attached to the ski only at the tip of the toe! Once you get balanced, the light swing weight of cross-country skis, which allows a quick edge change, is a delight.

We've found that the simplest way for alpiners to get an immediate feel for cross-country downhill is to find a packed slope and swing the skis around in a quick hockey stop. This gives an immediate feeling for the differences in the two types of equipment. It's also a good way to prove to yourself that you can do more than a snowplow on skinny skis.

Alpine getting worn for you? Ski area bumps too big? Need a new thrill at the old alpine game? Rent metal-edged nordic skis and head back to the lifts.

In Summary

In the end, of course, you need to refine your skills and maneuvers. After you do it enough, your legs remember patterns so you can move over the snow like a relative expert. Great skiers do things about the same ways as they move through snowy space. They balance comfortably atop overlong, flexing slats; they twist and turn elegantly; they edge their skis and push off against that edge. Nobody is a first-run natural, but all of us can learn to turn a profit on the hills and cash in on the free speed.

There will come a day when you will forget the individual moves of technique. That's what you're after. Then you have reached a level of skiing that is your own self-expression toward terrain and snow. Then you're as free as the gravity you've learned to trust, free from normal speed limits.

Top cross-country ski racers casually attain speeds of 30 miles an hour on skis weighing only 1,000 grams. Gillette once clocked in at 62 miles an hour on telemark skis. He strutted his stuff until news arrived several years later that a Frenchman rocketed down a speed skiing course at 101 miles an hour on extralong telemark skis. As they say in Vermont's Northeast Kingdom, "Now Ned, don't say nothin'."

Others do. "To me," says alpine ski great Stein Eriksen, "Gracefulness on skis should be the end-all of the sport."

CHAPTER 6

Telemark Skiing

*I*t is not uncommon to ride the lifts at a downhill resort these days and hear fellow riders calling out "Telemark!" to genuflecting rover packs of cross-country skiers charging down the slopes below. What they're asking for is a turn that's been around ever since skis were twelve feet long and attached to the shoes with thongs. Unlike other turns, in which feet are kept side by side, in the telemark a skier scissors the legs fore and aft, steering around on what is essentially one long ski. It's a graceful, flamboyant turn, the mark of the all-around cross-country stylist, and the only one you can't also do with alpine skis. This is the turn that makes the most of a loose heel.

It was in Norway, in the mid-1800s, that Sondre Norheim first wrapped twisted osier withes around his heel to gain more steering control, thus "inventing" the binding. From 1868 on, he and the ruffians from the Telemark region in southern Norway dominated ski competitions in Christiania (now Oslo) as the turn that Norheim developed in Telemark overshadowed the skidding, parallel Christiania turn. A half century ago modern alpine bindings, which clamped heels to skis, spelled the eclipse of the telemark turn, but only temporarily. Even as late as 1946, a ski manual stated, "Because of its narrow track and the minimum amount of snow displacement, the telemark requires less physical effort in deep snow than any other turn. This factor alone justifies its presence in a skier's bag of tricks."

The recent revival of the telemark is partly due to the switch-hitting of some of the best alpine skiers and partly to the introduction of more sophisticated metal-edged cross-country skis with alpine-like flexes and stiff boots. And the turn itself

Telemarking in British Columbia's Bugaboos

has changed a bit. No longer does the tip of the back ski passively nestle next to the instep of the front boot. The ski is still back but more nearly parallel, and carving. A top-notch telemark turn is aggressive, like a good alpine turn. Alpine, nordic, and mountaineering skiers alike have rediscovered the challenge, usefulness, and just plain fun of sweeping downhill leaving a single carved track.

Why Telemark?

Aside from the utility of the turn, telemarks have a low-rider appeal. As Todd Eastman of Lake Placid, New York, says, "the lower you get, the deeper the snow." What we're after is low-rider enjoyment. If a parallel is an upright turn, then the telemark is a downright turn—downright fun! Telemark anywhere, just because it feels good. Or be offhand about it: we've

Surf's up: banking a telemark in a smooth sweep

seen members of the University of Vermont cross-country ski team "tele" to a stop at the end of an interval training loop, instead of braking, as most skiers would, with a parallel hockey stop.

But a telemark is useful as well as fun; use it when you need fore and aft stability. In deep powder? Drop into a telemark, essentially putting yourself in one long ski for power steering par excellence. Frozen in a vicelike grip with your parallel stance in dense crud snow? Initiate a telemark with a step or two, or even a jump. It's quick. So too in tight trees. Even moguls. It's stable. No wonder ski jumpers land in a telemark position. If you're carrying a backpack, a smooth "tele" will not throw you down. It's a tolerant turn, this double-clutch shuffle, custom tailored for cross-country equipment.

Cross-country downhill has put a new spark into skiing, an uninhibited, fall-down-and-get-up-and-go spirit. It's a pure delight to swing with gravity on light equipment, switching from parallel to telemark as the terrain and snow dictate, just as we'd intermingle skating, diagonal and double-pole strides on the flat track.

Before You Arc

Skiing downhill is by no means a natural sport. It is not like walking, running, jumping, or throwing. It is very much a learned activity, one that takes sophisticated concentration and coordination. All our instincts tell us not to fall, not to lean out over the skis, not to speed. But we can all get the hang of it if we focus on the essentials. The balance demanded for telemarking at first seems that of a tightrope walker, the body position that of a rock star in the layout position, and the velocity that of a downhill racer—all on cross-country skis that look, to the neophyte, rather insubstantial in comparison to their obese alpine cousins. ("Why are my skis so thin?" said a friend, responding to a question from an alpine skier. "Madam, they've been sick.")

Chances are that you will have had some skiing expertise under your belt before you try your first telemark. As a cross-country skier, you must learn to entertain more speed and learn to carve through a turn. If you're an alpine skier, you must adjust to a different leg position. Even though the leg position may initially feel weird, the rhythm of the turns will be natural. You are working to overcome a mind problem more than a physical problem. Use the local ski area lifts to get mileage and to get accustomed to accelerating straight over into the fall line, to capture an easy balance, to turn left and right with equal expertise, and to prime those thigh muscles.

Telemark virtuoso Art Burrows of Aspen, Colorado, advises, "If you make a commitment, as I did a few years ago, to try to ski everything on cross-country skis, then you will get good. Then you will not have the alternative of retreating to alpine skis when it looks tough. You will press through and get better."

Body Position

A telemark is really only a super-duper, gravity-assisted diagonal stride. Head down to your local bowling alley and roll a set. The position you find yourself in as you release the ball is a hardwood telly. Position on your skis is the key ingredient when learning. Quick turns will come later.

Distribute your weight fifty-fifty between the front and back ski. Putting half your weight on your rear ski is going to feel like 80 percent at first. Think of squashing a bug under the

Proper body position is a fifty-fifty proposition.

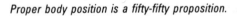

Don't do the D'Artagnan

ball of your back foot. (Avoid being up on tiptoe, making it impossible to exert pressure, and leading to tepid telemarking.) Pressure here will make the rear ski edge and carve instead of skid, giving rudderlike control. Tuck your rear leg under you so you're in an athletic position. Beginners are apt to do the D'Artagnan, lunging forward onto a bent front leg, back leg straight, as if skewering a seventeenth-century opponent.

Bend at the knees, not at the waist. To be centered over your skis means standing more erect than in alpine or flat-track cross-country skiing. Viewed from the side, a telemarker's shoulder, hip, and knee of the flexed back leg should be in a straight line. Keep your head up. Your body follows your head, so a droopy cranium hunches your upper body, transferring too much weight onto the front ski. Better to drive your hips in under you.

Keep your feet fairly close together fore and aft at first (no more than twelve inches apart), concentrating on knee bending. Feet working closely will feel familiar to alpine skiers and will prove easier for all beginning telemarkers to weight the skis equally. Touch the trailing knee to the calf of the leading leg to avoid too long a spread. Never allow your rear leg to straighten.

Ratify the Neutrality Act between Legs and Upper Body,

Drive the inside hand; if it lags back, so will you . . . down and out.

securing an enduring Peace of the Torso. Keep it quiet up top, especially with a backpack; hands low for optimum center of gravity. Balance is difficult at first. You'll tend to lift up your hands and jab your poles in busily to stay upright, looking like a great square-rigged ship. Well and good to use outriggers as a training crutch, but this banging about will upset your rhythm, expend lots of energy, and eliminate any aggressiveness. Collapse that umbrella you appear to be holding over your head and let yourself down on your skis. To quiet your arms, think of gripping the handles of your poles lightly. To get your arms low when learning, consider using very short poles, some twenty centimeters shorter than normal cross-country poles.

Concentrate on driving the inside hand (arm opposite the forward leg) to keep you square on your skis. It is a compensating factor for the rear leg. When you turn, hold the inside (uphill) hand dynamically forward to offset centrifugal force and to cancel a tendency to overrotate (the forward ski a too heavily weighted pivot point) and spin out crazily at the end of

Half Court Telly: Here's a stunt Dostal picked up from cross-country guru and tennis pro manque John Caldwell—a recognized champion of the telemark turn. And just in time, as Dostal was headed for some high-angle 3-pin skiing in the Argentine Andes in August. Obviously, a time when gringo telly muscles were at their slackest. But a quick tone-up was secured by more time on the tennis courts. With his very good friend Charlie the tennis pro obligingly hitting balls at his feet, Dostal was forced into grueling half vollies. These thigh-straining shoe-top swats proved to be surprising and useful approximations of drop-down, nimble-footed jump telemarks.

each turn. Remember your diagonal stride, the dynamics of which are retained by thrusting your hips through. Commit to the turn, then sink and weight both skis.

Planting the Pole

With long-radius high-speed steered turns, less unweighting is needed, so it is not necessary to plant your poles. Just shift ski lead, lean into the turn, and go with the speed. But you'll want to plant the downhill pole when doing sharper, quicker telemarks, thereby creating a stable platform from which to rise up, unweight, and roll your knees to start the turn. It initiates the lead change of the skis. Plant the pole so it is

In telemark, as in parallel skiing, planting the pole triggers the turn.

synced with this briefly parallel and compact stance. Planting the pole also sets you facing down the hill with your upper body coiled, or torqued, in anticipation of the coming turn. Use your hips to help tip the skis onto their edges and keep them on edge. Let your hips rotate with the turning skis, but keep your torso facing down the hill so you're ready to be released into the next turn.

Garland

Pressing into a turn

First Turn

For the time being, forget about your poles.

Standing in place, familiarize yourself with the telemark position by sliding your skis back and forth like a diagonal stride, bending your knees and switching the lead ski. Discover that your weight feels best when equal on both skis.

Now it's time to move. Stride slightly downhill across an easy, groomed slope in the familiar rhythm of your diagonal stride, sinking into a telemark position with each stride. After three or four strides, push your *downhill* ski forward, genuflect, and do one turn up into the slope. Repeat, making a garland.

Now turn down the hill. This will involve a bit more speed. Once again stride across the hill in a shallow traverse. This time slide your *uphill* ski forward, stand on its inside edge, genuflect, press on both skis continually, and steer all the way around through the fall line with your front knee. There's your first real telemark.

It's important to finish your turns. Emphasize edging and

Most common mistake for downhill skier switching to telemark: no pressure on the back ski

weighting your rear ski, so you control it, and it works for you (and you don't spin out at the end of each turn). How? Press down on the *little toe* of your back foot. That one little thing makes all the difference. It improves edging and reduces skidding out of the rear ski. To feel that edging even more, press down on the big toe of your front foot. Now, *both* skis are working for you.

Remember the three keys while learning: (a) 50 percent of your weight on the rear foot; (b) keep your feet close together fore and aft; (c) drive the inside hand. Do these, and you'll elude half the telemark's sitzmarks. A loose-heeled binding means you cannot exert forward pressure on the tip of the ski, as in alpine, so you must sit squarely on the skis and use the maximum sidecut underfoot for turning. Pressure the ski into doing the work for you. Skis must really bend to turn—a curved object tends to follow an arced path.

Todd Eastman would ask you to exaggerate your breathing to get through a turn. Inhale as you come into the turn. This raises you a little off your skis (unweighting to initiate). Exhale as you sink into the turn. Think of everything dropping down, getting heavier as buoyant air is expelled.

Try these tricks to learn faster:

Bunny-hop: Can't get that feeling of committing into the turn? Wayne Hansen of Jackson, Wyoming, gets his students to hop to it. Traverse across an easy slope, then hop up into the air and land in a telemark stance. On each rhythmic hop switch ski

Bunny hop

leads. Finally, on the third or fourth hop, land and, in the same motion, press around in a telemark turn.

Rock and roll: Your first telemark may be a project on the skids, sliding out rather than carving. You want driving thrust out onto the front ski, followed by a quick rock back and drop down with weight on the rear ski to edge through the turn.

Rock and roll

Here's a way to get the feeling: during a shallow traverse across the hill, put your weight (as you normally would) on the downhill ski. Now pick the tip of the uphill ski up off the snow, then step forward and around into the fall line. (Lifting the *tip* of the ski rocks you back enough to force a concentration of weight onto the back ski, so it will carve.) Sink and press through the turn, allowing the rear ski to come in close to the steering front ski, riding them both. Rocking back puts weight on the rear ski. The roll forward catapults you into the turn. The step brings you through the fall line quickly, controlling speed. In the turn, both skis are weighted and carving a single arc, and hips are thrust into the turn.

The tightrope: Keeping yourself facing generally down the hill makes turning quicker and prevents overrotation. Twist-

The Tightrope

Heavy Hands

ing at the waist also automatically weights and edges the rear ski so it will carve for you early in the turn and not leave you behind. To get the sensation of facing downhill and anticipating, hold your poles in front as a tightrope walker would, then make several turns, trying to keep the poles across the hill at all times.

Heavy hands: Especially on harder snow, you'll want to thrust, or flex, your knees sideways into the hill to steer and edge. Compensate by bending your upper body out, away from the hill and over your feet in an angulated, comma shape. Your weight is then directly on your feet, yet ski edges are biting. Now if you hit a slick icy spot, your skis will not fly out from under you as they might if you banked the turn. To get the feel of this body position, Rick Borkovec of Crested Butte, Colorado, says to press the downhill (outside) hand in and down, toward the heel of the back foot to feel the angled body position.

Wedge telemark: You can also work from the familiar wedge to learn the telemark. Initiating the turn in a wedge stabi-

Starting a telemark from a familiar wedge

Staying in a wedge invites a fall.

lizes you. Think of it as a two-step sequential turn: first you stem the front ski, then you transfer your weight to the rear ski. Once you've steered through the fall line, bring your skis together with both skis working for you.

Cut the stem: As speed and confidence increase, cut down the angle (stemming stance) between the skis, so they slice. To do this, increase the radius or speed of the turn, or initiate it from a parallel stance. Staying in a wedge too long during the turn means each ski follows a different arc, cancelling the steering action. When the wedge is eliminated, the telemark becomes truly a steered turn.

Step telemark

Stepping is one way to initiate the turn. (Later you'll use it for short, quick turns in moguls, crud snow, and steep terrain. Its quick direction change allows you to "walk" down formidable slopes.) It commits your front foot to the turn and starts the steering ski turning through the fall line. Think of driving that front ski forward through the turn like a diagonal stride. But as soon as the turn takes place, weight the feet equally. Squeeze down onto the back foot smoothly so the rear ski becomes useful in edging and carving for control. Think of pressing down the *little toe* of the rear foot. This automatically edges the back ski. Using the rear ski makes the telemark useful as well as pretty.

Moguls: Beaver houses left over after sharp-toothed devastation? No, moguls are the bumpy residue of quickturning alpine skiers at lift-served areas. You can surely ski them with a parallel technique, staying low in your knees and rolling through the humpy terrain, but telemarking is another challenge altogether. It takes a lot of practice to avoid being choppy, but it's worth it. Use a modification of the step telemark.

In a telemark position, think of being on one long

Quick lead changes while telemarking in the bumps

articulating ski, progressing like a rubber boat undulating down whitewater rapids. You have the ultimately flexible ski which can bend like a universal joint, in the middle, to conform to the bumps, actually wrapping around each one. The key is timing, that ability to turn at the right place in the moguls so you don't crash into a mogul wall or clip your ski tails against a neighboring hillock. Change your lead ski on the top of the big bumps by springing into the air and landing with the front ski over the crest of the bump, then sinking and carving. Smaller bumps require only knee absorption during the lead change. A step telly with a hop is often a quick way to get around. And a double-pole plant helps rapid-fire unweighting. Come down hard on the front part of your ski (on the ball of your foot) to really set your edges and control speed. You must lean forward and commit as if sacrificing yourself to gravity. Work into and around the backside of each mogul, for it is here that you discover soft, forgiving snow.

Give your rear leg a bit of consideration now that your knee is cranked down close to the snow. A hidden rock or stump can devastate an innocent knee cap. Wear plastic hockey knee pads for protection if you're going to go for any amount of speed. And use safety straps to prevent a runaway ski should the binding release.

Linking Turns

Ultimately aim for connecting turns. It is the *rhythm* of telemarking that skiers find exquisitely natural, like the smooth grace of the diagonal stride, one motion leading into the next. As you rise between turns, keep both skis flat during the lead change. Only edge both skis after the correct foot is forward for the next turn. Linking makes your turns not only easier but more dynamic and utilitarian in all types of snow. Long, hesitant traverses between turns destroy cadence and strain your thigh muscles. The beauty lies in repeating the arc. Above all, follow gravity and red-line the fun meter.

Speed for Ease

For long radius telemarks on groomed slopes and in light powder, you don't need the step once you get used to the acceleration. It actually gets easier with speed, but you have to put

Step through for quick turning.

The lure of the telemark: the lower you get, the deeper the snow

yourself in the fall line and love it. "You must attain the maximum velocity to create the necessary resistance," deadpans Art Burrows, "then just stand there and arc. It's truly energy conserving." With speed, you just cruise, gently rising up and down with each turn, edging in alternate directions as you shift skis fore and aft. Speed allows a more parallel telemark. Slower telemarks are more like a stem or step maneuver.

The key to these long, steered turns without a step is pressing more weight on the back ski as speed increases. Timing is critical. Start shifting your weight early onto the inside ski just before the turn. Otherwise you'll get on what will be the rear ski too late. You'll lose the carving power of the rear ski, and the turn will be dead.

Telemark Racing

Competition is the logical extension of most sporting pastimes, and telemarking is no exception. In the late 1970s a group of ex-alpine racers in Colorado, already expert back-country telemarkers, established the Summit Telemark Series. Wool knickers, touring boots, and long, deep sweeping tellies were the order of the day.

Today the standards of competition have risen drastically. The best racers look like aggressive Alpine World Cup

Running gates in the North American Championship

champions and practice their gates daily. Races are held throughout the country. The spectator no longer sees any wool. Rather, he sees sleek nylon racing suits, high-top leather and plastic boots and metal-edged skis with alpine flex characteristics specifically designed for racing. Even with these serious accouterments, telemark racing has kept its fun-loving, know-everyone-else-on-the-circuit atmosphere. Races are run on dual giant slalom courses, with elimination rounds, competitors going head-to-head.

The rules of telemark racing require that the racer *execute* his turn as a telemark (no matter how brief). He is not required to pass through the gate in a telemark. Most good racers have completed their turn above the gate. They hit an instantaneous, sharp, powerful telemark, then fire on in a parallel position until the next turn. Gatekeepers assess time penalties for each nontelemark turn. The speed of the top guns is fantastic. High-level racing is attractive for a select few. Running gates, regardless of the speed you wish to go, improves your skiing. It helps your ability to turn at will, putting you more in control. It keeps you honest: everything must be precisely executed at higher speeds and higher pulse rates.

CHAPTER 7

Equipment

*T*here are a few key strategies in determining which cross-country ski equipment will best suit you and enhance your skiing. You can make some gross approximations of what you need in skis, poles, boots, and bindings by asking a few questions right off. Will you ski primarily in machine-groomed tracks, or will you break your own trail? No one ski can do it all. Are you willing to learn how to wax a ski for proven performance? Or will you sacrifice a little fine tuning for wax-less convenience? Is cross-country skiing going to be a major winter pursuit? If so, you'll want gear that will still be service-able after you've developed some skills; after all, if you're reasonably athletic, you won't be a beginner for more than a half-dozen outings.

With that in mind, don't buy cheap. Cross-country equipment is most often sold in packages. There are some legitimate values here but avoid the $99 special. The hook in package deals is usually an attractive ski. But the quality of the boots, bindings, and poles that complete the package should be com-mensurate. If you're a cross-country skier, you also may be a runner or a hiker. Do you pursue these sports in $20 chain-store shoes? How long would you stick with tennis outfitted with a $25 prestrung racket?

But first, try before you buy. We know you've heard this before. But you wouldn't buy a car any other way. Granted, this will be more difficult if your roost is down country rather than in snow country. You're most likely to find demo programs—usually at no charge—at snow-belt specialty shops and ski cen-ters. Another good bet are "demo days" staged throughout the

Proper equipment can determine your on-snow star quality.

season by equipment sales representatives at ski areas.

Newcomers to skiing are often surprised at how sensitive they are to differences in relatively unfamiliar equipment. But you can feel a difference of one hundred or two hundred grams in a ski. Even without a ski tester's vocabulary, you'll feel which skis are dead underfoot and which send you skimming. The same goes for different length ski poles. Test one category at a time. Trying high-performance track skis and backcountry skis together will give a feel for the differences in their gross design characteristics, but will lead to confusion in settling on a particular model. The quickest way to form an opinion is to try a different ski *in the same category* on each foot, a different pole in each hand—much better than trying successive pairs. After taking them on the flats and uphill to narrow your choice between skis, run pairs downhill to see how they turn.

Skis

Waxless or waxable: There has to be something on the base of a ski to give you grip. On waxable skis, snow crystals penetrate the wax of proper consistency, resulting in grip. Emphasis on proper; you have to match the wax to the temperature

Skiing is still fun whether on hand-carved Manchurian skis...

... or on the latest high-tech for kids.

Indifferent route-finding can have a devastating effect on equipment.

and the snow conditions, or it's no go. In powder snow or spring snow making the match is pretty easy, and the glide is great. On waxless skis, the mechanical pattern on the bottom of the ski is configured to dig in when pressed into the snow, but it offers less resistance as the ski slides forward—like traditional climbing skins. Patterns keep the bases from being entirely smooth, which limits performance. The skis don't slide as easily through a turn as waxable skis or glide as easily down the track. And some waxless patterns work better than others on different kinds of snow. As Harald Bjerke of Swix Sport (a major wax manufacturer) says, "Remember that using a waxless ski is like playing eighteen holes of golf with only the putter." Few waxless skis work well on hard or icy snow, and you can't adjust to the snow as with waxable skis. When snow falls right around the freezing point—giving those who wax their skis fits—waxless skis are best of show. If you live in an area where changeable snow conditions are the norm, like the mountains of California and the Pacific Northwest, take a long look at waxless skis.

There are some waxless skis that have smooth bottoms that don't wear out, glide well, turn well, and have base patterns that are similar to the average-size snow crystals and change-able according to conditions. Pursuit of this ultimate waxless ski is, if you will, the ski industry's Philosophers' Stone. Such skis have come, gone, and returned recently as "chemical base" skis. But they require some attention from sandpapers and silicon preparations and have yet to be recognized as the final solution.

Indeed, despite the hype about convenience, waxless skis are not maintenance free, unless you want to tolerate steadily deteriorating performance. Think of them not so much as wax-less skis but "less wax" skis, suggests Swix's Ole Rostad. If they have high-quality plastic bases, like waxable skis, an occa-sional hot waxing on tips and tails with a glider wax will markedly improve their gliding; that's less work for you. If even a minimal hot waxing is unappealing, at least take the ten sec-onds required to wipe or spray on a lubricating preparation. Not only will bottoms be faster, but they will be less likely to clog up with snow that, at 32 degrees Fahrenheit, can stick even to wax-less bases and leave you doing the Cakewalk. And waxless skis can get dirty, especially in spring snow when they pick up sludge and pine needles from the snowpack and wax from other skis. A rag, some wax solvent, and another five minutes is all you need for a noticeable improvement in performance.

In track or out: The tracks molded into machine-groomed snow at most ski areas let you fly like never before. For this you need a whippet of a ski. It should be light, so you can conserve energy, and narrow, so it doesn't drag against the side of the track and slow you down. The tip should be flexible so that the ski will slither around curves in the tracks. (Get a feeling for this by pulling it straight back toward you and by twisting it.) Not surprisingly, then, you'll find a lot of people using racing skis. But they're not necessarily racers any more than those who ride twelve-speed bikes or drive sports cars.

Racing skis are about forty-four-millimeters wide and have soft tips and a parallel shape. Hold one up to a ski for off-track skiing, and the differences will become apparent. The off-track or touring ski has *sidecut*. Widest at the tip, it narrows at the center and flares again at the tail. That makes it easier to turn. The in-track ski gets its turnability from a softer, more flex-ible tip, which also provides the shock absorption necessary for a smooth ride. But put it in unpacked, off-track snow, and it's too flexible and narrow to provide much of a platform for either

Tips tell the tale: from left, telemark ski, touring ski, traditional striding ski, skating ski.

striding or turning. It lacks sufficient flotation. In contrast, the wider (fifty millimeter or so) touring ski with sidecut that planes in loose snow will feel clunky in the track and slower due to heavier weight.

For in-track skiing, there are other choices besides a full-fledged racer. De-tuned racers are slightly heavier and some-times a bit wider; just a few years ago, many of them would have been top-of-the-line racing skis. Many manufacturers make so-called performance or sport skis, which have most of the features of the racing skis, but with a little more sidecut. This makes them somewhat better out-of-track performers, but to us they are primarily track skis.

Backcountry and metal edge: Just because you're skiing in unbroken snow doesn't mean you need a metal-edged ski. Indeed, the addition of metal edges adds weight to a ski, because there must be increased width and stiffness for them to work. (A metal edge on a racing ski wouldn't turn it into a back-country performer.) All of which may turn a scamper through untracked powder on rolling terrain into a slog. But if you ski on steep, difficult terrain, the edges may be vital. It follows that in trying out edged skis, how they turn is paramount. Skis with stiffer tips will tend to hold better on harder snow. But the ski that's such a stable platform for cruising in well-packed western snow may turn into something of a rogue submarine in late-season eastern slush, diving and surfacing with a will of its own. As with track skis, the more you ski, the more sensitive you'll become to ski design and performance.

Skating skis: Welcome to the frontier of ski design. Skis specifically designed for skating have been around for only a few years. But even before that, snow skaters had a feel for what they needed and took matters into their own hands. Right off, shorter skis made for less entanglement. So in wild fits of *circumskision*, the hacksaws came out to crop the tips and tails. Then manufacturers caught up. They made skis shorter, but stiffer to support the weight of a skier normally on a ski ten centimeters longer. Since skaters don't ski in tracks, there's no need for the high, curving tip; blunt and bobbed is less likely to catch on loose snow. Because skating is partly an edging movement, ski sidewalls are reinforced. And because skaters push out as well as down, the forebody of the ski is more torsionally rigid—more like a backcountry ski.

When you take skating skis out for a test spin, you'll notice a few things. If the tip isn't rigid enough, it will slide out to the side, especially on uphills. Since you're not in the tracks that normally guide a ski, the ski's ability to track on smooth snow is important. On this point there's no unanimity in design; some skis have side cut to enhance tracking, others have multiple grooves like a straight-running ski for jumping. These multiple grooves can somewhat inhibit the ski's readiness to turn. Take that into consideration if you plan to tour on skating skis.

With skiers understandably asking if they need another pair of skis to skate on, manufacturers have produced so-called combi skis that incorporate in their design some elements of a striding ski—notably the overall flex—along with the bobbed and stiffer tip of skating skis. They are usually sized five centimeters shorter than a striding ski. As with any compromise, you give a little and get a little: Combis are an answer but not the best for either technique.

Fitting skis: Beware of the hoary "ski-tip-to-the-upraised-palm" method. If you have an overhead light bulb to change, the stretch will do you good; but you'll probably get an overlong ski. Most men will ski a 210-centimeter ski for striding; women will go with one of 190–200 centimeters. More important than your height is your weight. Stiffness is crucial. No matter whether it's waxable or waxless or even a skater, if the ski's too stiff, you'll spin four wheels on uphills, unable to get the whole ski onto the snow. Skis that are too flexible or "soft" will cause

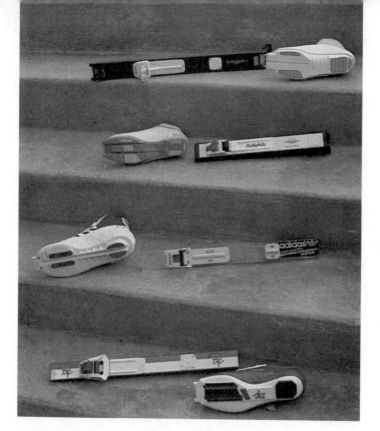

Despite design differences, with ridge plates and matching grooves, system boots are sole mates.

wax to wear off all too quickly; beyond that, you'll feel like you are driving on an underinflated tire or pushing them through sand. The suitability of performance skis depends, increasingly, on your weight. This is less true on skis for out-of-track skiing. Generally speaking, if you can just squeeze skis together, base to base, you're likely to have a suitable pair.

Beyond that, though, check to see if the skis match up. Hold them in front of a light source and press bottoms together as you sight down their length. Reject pairs that seem to separate except in the midsection. Either they could be slow because of hard spots or squirrely going downhill.

Boots

Boots are the most important piece of cross-country ski equipment you'll buy. After all, you're not going to get blistered

Armored personnel carriers: higher-cut, stiffened boots for skating... and more

feet from the *ski.*

Choose a boot that feels like your tennis or running shoe. Skiers often go too roomy and wind up partway through the season with sloppy boots. Don't hesitate to fine tune your fit by substituting a thicker or thinner sockliner or foot bed for the one supplied. It's better than cramming in extra socks. In addition to walking around in the boots, clip into the demo board on which the bindings are mounted to check the flex.

Don't get more boot than you need. You don't need a high, heavy boot, stiff enough for lift-served telemark skiing, if you're pushing a wide, light, and edgeless touring ski over easy, rolling terrain. A better choice would be a "cruiser weight"—a lighter boot with a torsionally rigid sole (thanks to running-shoe technology) for real turning power.

Seventy-fives: Until about a decade ago, there wasn't much ado about boots. For skiing on trails or easy off-track terrain, there was a leather brogan with a projecting Donald Duck toe that clamped down over three pins on the binding plate.

(This traditional boot and binding gave cross-country the name three-pin skiing.) Eventually, the width of the toe and the binding were standardized at seventy-five millimeters—the so-called Nordic Norm.

The seventy-fives function in several ways. They are laterally stiff for control, yet flexible enough fore and aft to allow for a comfortable stride. They also offer support and warmth. But there are disadvantages. To build stiffness into a leather boot, you have to add weight. And a binding that clamps down in front of the toes often jams the toes.

Backcountry skiing is still the province of seventy-five-millimeter boots. This is partly because the "wings" of the binding provide extra support in turning, and partly because the boots themselves are often so heavily reinforced. There's also the security of the rubber lug sole for stretches of hiking and rock scrambling.

Over heavy boots, gaiters that fully cover the boots offer complete protection, especially in wet snow. A rubber rand stretches tightly around the boot's welt—where the upper meets the sole. Remember to pull it up at the front when storing the boots lest its pressure on the empty boot turn the toes up in a medieval and thoroughly uncomfortable curl.

Boots for backcountry: cruiserweights top, dreadnaughts bottom

Systems boots: Technology has caught up with boots and bindings, just as it had with skis and poles. The new systems boots and bindings parcel out the functions that were formerly incorporated in the seventy-five millimeter boot. The new designs, however, mean an end to interchangeability. Despite the bells and whistles in the designs of the established systems, when you look under the hood, they are more similar than different. Snub-nose plastic soles are fitted with a metal pin that clamps into the binding housing. We're talking here about nothing more complicated than a door hinge. Without a spring, though, a door would flap freely; so would skis. So either a spring or a rubber plug snaps the ski back to the boot. The elasticity of these flex bits governs how much forward flex you get. There are usually three or four different stiffnesses available, so you can get just the right feel.

Now that flex is more a function of the binding, boot soles are made of plastic that is torsionally more rigid. In the sole, a longitudinal groove mates with a steering ridge that is nailed to the ski. You can use the whole foot for turning, which is a big improvement in control. Boot uppers are usually of lighter, insulated fabric and synthetics. Some have a boot-within-a-boot design that cinches the foot in for further control and another layer for coverage.

The advantages of these new designs are so compelling that for in-track skiing, we can't envision a skier who wouldn't be swayed. One caveat, though: about half of the boots, from different manufacturers, have a rubber rather than plastic sole (thought to give better traction and warmth to "tourers" or the slower-paced crowd). But this sole is inherently less rigid torsionally. And without a substantial shank and insole, sometimes barely adequate in cheaper models, your heel can torque right off the ski—a major problem in the old seventy-fives especially for those with large feet. So make sure you get systems performance along with systems features.

Skating boots: In the balance game that is skating, being able to ride a gliding ski is paramount. It won't do to have the foot collapsing inward (pronating) or outward (supinating). It is no surprise that skating boots became externally stiffened and higher cut to counteract these tendencies. Still, whatever the design, the boot first must fit comfortably and snugly. Beyond that, low cut, high cut—it depends on your skiing. The boot design shouldn't impede your range of motion.

The most interesting thing about skate boots has little to do with skating. Skiers of modest ability are now picking up on the higher, reinforced boots because of the downhill control they offer. Molded plastic supports are coming quickly into boots for the full range of skiing.

Poles

It was only about a decade ago that buying ski poles was little more than an automatic process. Racers got aluminum; tourers and recreational skiers, tonkin cane. We're talking shaft material here, and that was about all that mattered. Regretably, non-racers got the shaft in other ways: badly designed handles, poorly attached baskets, and low-grade leather straps.

Happily, that's changed. Poles are now a best buy in cross-country equipment and improvements in their design have kept up with those in skis and boots.

Poles for track skiing have a canted, anatomically contoured handle—usually of plastic—courtesy of racing technology. And along with that comes an easily adjustable nylon strap.

Tonkin or bamboo has disappeared as a material for shafts. Most inexpensive poles have shafts of fiberglass or aluminum. In some cases, the latter may have less strength than cheap lawn furniture. The stronger and stiffer the shaft, the better it is. You don't want the shaft to deflect and absorb energy that should be pushing you forward.

And, while the basket makes a bit of a difference, pole shafts determine the swing weight, or balance. As with any tool—golf club, tennis racket, hammer, or chainsaw—balance contributes to efficiency. Better ski poles have more weight near the handle, thanks to a shaft that tapers to the basket. The very best poles are so light and well balanced that you'll feel as if you're swinging forward little more than your hand. A cheap, poorly balanced pole will feel as if you're swinging a lantern.

Baskets used to come one way—round. They are still that way for touring and backcountry poles, where you need the flotation in unbroken snow. But in the tracks, that front half of the round basket tended to lever the pole out of the snow as you pushed down and back. So racing poles acquired a half basket. It's a feature that appears—or should—on just about all poles for track skiing, including recreational. But what if you might like a little off-track skiing? There's a compromise—an elliptical basket with a bit more projection in front.

In the realm of racing poles, you're paying for shafts stiffened and strengthened with carbon fiber and Kevlar. As with skis, so with poles: If you're an eager exercise skier who skis in tracks, you'll appreciate the features of a racing pole. You can get these features in less than full-race poles that substitute or mix in slightly cheaper shaft materials like fiberglass in the shafts.

Skating has taken poles to new lengths and prices. It's now possible to pay almost as much for a pair of poles as for a top-of-the-line pair of racing skis. Making a light, stiff shaft in a 140-centimeter length is one thing; doing it in a 170-centimeter length is another—and more expensive—proposition.

Skating's also made a difference in the ways poles are fitted. For this new technique, poles should be up to the chin or nose. For the traditional diagonal technique, poles have been fitted to the armpit. But a longer pole here has proven more efficient, and fitting to the top of the shoulder now seems to be finding favor.

As one Finnish ski team member said just before the last Olympics, "I can't believe we skied with such short poles for so long." He was talking about poles for striding. If you decide to try a longer pole for traditional skiing, you'll know that you've gone too far if your upper body starts to move up and down in order to get the pole clear of the snow. The pole basket may even bounce against the snow on recovery—a sure sign of excess.

Skating has also wrought a big change in pole grips. Essentially, poles have been held the same way since skiers went from a single long pole to the familiar pair with handle and strap, a hundred years ago. You grasped the handle and pushed against the strap as if hanging onto a climbing rope.

Recently, new designs have changed the attitude of the hand on the pole grip—as if you were holding the rungs of a ladder. The argument goes that more large muscles of the side and shoulder are recruited for more power in both skating and even striding. These designs bear watching. If racers switch over, it's a sure sign that the new designs will probably help any skier.

Poles for touring and backcountry skiing have also received a make-over. More are now adjustable, anywhere from 100 centimeters to 150 centimeters. To us, they are eminently

Coming to grips with new designs

useful. Crank them up full-length for skating across a snowed-over lake. Crank them down for descents. On steep traverses, shorten the uphill pole and lengthen the downhill one for better balance. The weak link in adjustable poles is the internal screw-down nut or cam; if a pole breaks it's likely to be there. When we use adjustable poles, a pole repair sleeve goes along.

Packs

Skiing with a pack is never as pleasant as skiing free, but for all-day tours it is necessary to bring along extra clothing, waxes, map, sunglasses, water, and a few things to eat; as well as a spare tip in case of a broken ski, space blanket, and matches for emergencies. Include tape—adhesive tape for blisters and fiberglass strapping tape for repairing broken equipment. Tape is an instant all-inclusive repair kit. (People have even been known to tape bindings back onto skis or a broken or delaminated boot right to the ski!)

A good-sized fanny pack may well be all you need for fast tours close to home, since it hinders skiing movement very

Pick a pack that fits close lest you be in a pickle on the steeps.

little. But for ventures farther afield, you'll want a bit more capacity. We prefer a day pack that is fairly tall but not too wide, so arms can swing freely. We've found that most climbing rucksacks are a pretty good bet: they'll provide enough capacity so you don't have to cram everything in so tightly that you end up with a tight "ball" on your back, which is uncomfortable.

The problem on multiday treks of course is how to carry all the gear and still enjoy the experience. The first step is to choose a large pack that is comfortable, stable, and simply designed. Most designers get carried away with the process of designing and forget that serious backpackers want only what is necessary out on the trail. Remember that you'll be operating cords and buckles on the trail with cold hands or mittens. Intricate systems often let you down when you most need them. For control while touring, stay away from packs that roll with every skiing movement. Choose one of the specially designed soft packs or interior-frame packs that "cling" to your body. This is especially critical in downhill skiing situations where a loose pack will exaggerate any error you commit, often throwing you off balance and leading to bruising or dangerous falls. The totally soft packs are more stable but more difficult to pack. The manner in which they are packed forms the frame. Be careful not to have hard objects jabbing into your back.

We like soft packs best for medium-weight loads. For heavy and larger loads on extensive tours, go with an interior-frame pack which helps distribute the load more comfortably. Important for ease of carrying loads is a sophisticated yet simple arrangement by which an auxiliary strap "picks" the weight up off your shoulder straps, thereby lessening the pressure on your shoulders, especially while poling. (The trade-off here is that the pack tends to sway a bit more.) A sternum strap which links the two shoulder straps across the chest further frees shoulder movement and eliminates sway. Make sure all straps can be adjusted while you are skiing. A wide waist belt, which is padded at the hips and easily closed by Velcro or quick-release buckle, further fastens the pack so it almost becomes part of your body and moves with it.

Make sure that pockets are removable so you can use the pack for faster skiing and complete poling extension if you wish. Side straps, which can be used to carry skis on your pack, are useful in case you have to walk the last couple of miles of the tour. Compartmentalize your gear by packing certain similar things in nylon stuff sacks and labeling each. In this way you'll maintain some order when unpacking at your campsite. Pack heavy items low and closest to your back for maximum stability. Items needed during the day should be placed on top for easy access.

As you might suspect, to ski with a heavy backpack you'll

When you can't hang another pack on your body, you can still attach a sled.

have to make considerable adjustments in your technique. But before that, adjust the pack itself. Cinch it down packhorse tight before downhills to eliminate sway. You'll feel temporarily constricted, but you and the pack will turn as one. Gillette recalls starting off around Mount McKinley with eighty pounds on his back (his skis were only forty-seven-millimeters wide, and he used three-pin bindings). At first he could barely support the load, to say nothing of moving forward or negotiating downhills.

Weight on your back accentuates any mistake, so the key is not to make any mistakes. Ski very conservatively with a heavy pack, often electing to make a series of traverses down a slope rather than link turns. Unless you require additional pushing power uphill, use your poles relatively little in comparison to skiing without a pack and keep your hands low as if you're walking. Since packs press down on the muscles running across the top of the shoulders, raising the hands high in front brings fatigue faster. Falling with the persuasion of a big pack is never subtle. Try your utmost to maintain your balance, but when all is obviously lost, let go and relax, trying to avoid jamming head and shoulders into hard snow or rocks. Gillette's McKinley trip very nearly had to be aborted after Allan Bard dislocated a shoulder in a fall that was vicious only because of the weight he carried.

Sleds

During Gillette's High Arctic Expedition to Ellesmere Island each man hauled his gear in an eight-foot fiberglass sled. It was the only practical means of transporting 240 pounds apiece. They got the sleds through chaotic ocean pack ice, up steep glacier tongues, and down rocky river valleys. Of course you must choose your route carefully—certain terrain eliminates sled hauling—but consider a sled as a practical alternative to humping heavy backpacks. We prefer boat-type sleds which float on the snow and have angled sides to prevent capsizing in deep snow. Long sleds tend to even out small terrain variations. Rigid fiberglass pulling poles control the sled effectively; some come equipped with springs at the junction to the waist belt for easier striding action. We prefer a chest-shoulder-and-waist-combination pulling harness.

Other uses for sleds are for toting the small kids on a tour

Skiers generate enough heat to turn themselves into a human geyser field.

or packing supplies into a hunting or fishing camp or off-the-road homestead.

Ski Bags

Bags for your skis are often an overlooked necessity. Why leave your skis exposed on your ski rack and have them prepped—corrosively—by the department of highways as you head for the snow? If you're flying, realize that you have to armor your skis. Get an oversize bag, big enough for a couple of pairs of skis (and poles) with a full-length, heavy zipper. Then treat it like a suitcase, stuffing in boots and ski clothes around your skis and poles until it's nearly drum tight. Some skiers will even bag their delicate high-performance poles separately within their ski bag before packing, to avoid, as one observer said, having to learn to ski one-handed at their destination.

Clothing

Selecting the right clothing is as important to the success of a tour or race as is matching a ski to the snow and terrain you'll encounter.

How much to wear: Overdressing is the most common mistake. Cross-country skiing is the eminent self-warming winter pursuit. You need fewer clothes than you may think. (A recent Canadian study found that the amount of clothing needed to keep you warm sitting in a seventy-degree room is the same needed for walking at forty degrees or running at five below zero.) Still, on a cold but not frigid morning, it's not uncommon to see inexperienced skiers appear to be dressed for an assault on the West Ridge of Everest. This down-filled quilted excess simply won't do. Not only is it difficult to ski when overdressed, it guarantees an immediate overheating of your engine and a sloshing sweat bath.

The secret is to layer so you can tailor your dress to the needs of the moment according to the demands of exertion and weather. Rather than one heavy layer of clothing, you should aim for several layers of lighter items. These different layers trap the warmth your body produces. (Clothing fibers do not insulate; it's the trapped air in and between layers.) Layering enables you to remove a veneer or two to allow heat and moisture to escape. When you rest for an extended period and start to cool down, simply compensate by putting on extra layers. Consider how uncomfortably you would sleep if you utilized only one great down quilt all year round.

The bottom line: if you're slightly chilly as you start off, you've probably got just enough on. You'll warm up quickly.

Downhillers taking a day off at a cross-country area are hands-down favorites for getting overheated. It's often because they have little experience with cross-country, and their clothing is limited to what they brought for lift-served skiing. You don't need it all—not the insulated bibs *and* the heavy long underwear. Not the turtleneck, the sweater, *and* the insulated jacket. If options are limited, at least eliminate a layer. And make liberal use of zippers. It's better to take along garments you'd normally use for spring skiing, such as wind shirts and pants.

Your clothing should fit your body without pressing or binding in any one place, making it uncomfortable or reducing the blood supply to your extremities. It should be designed to allow freedom of movement. It should be of breathable material so your body moisture can escape, but tightly woven so water and snow will roll off and wind will be cut. "Light is right," since insulation is proportional to thickness, not weight. Check that your clothing covers the critical freezing points: head, neck, wrists, waist, ankles. And above all, adjust it immediately if you're too hot or cold.

Chances are that if you ski cross-country you're probably active in other sports and have a closetful of clothes already suitable for winter outings. The sports clothing industry is already pumping out such multipurpose, flexible wear. We recently heard one veteran skier tell less-experienced companions that dressing for cross-country skiing was not all that arcane: "It's like winter bicycling," he said, right on the mark.

Underwear: Bicycling and other outdoor sports quickly borrowed from cross-country skiing what has become a staple: so-called "transport" underwear. When putting together your on-snow wardrobe, start with transport. Sweating can reduce the insulative value of your clothing to 10 percent of its original value. But this stuff doesn't stay wet. Moisture is pushed through to the next layer.

Polypropylene was the first fabric to appear. It's plastic, but woven to have the look and feel of cotton. A trendy mail-order catalog recently inveighed against work-out clothes "clogged with synthetics." But we say, Give It Your Oil. Polypropylene and other petroleum derivatives such as treated polyester keep a dry layer next to your skin (although they do it

Circa 1972: Gillette natty in the organic, pre-synthetic days

in slightly different ways). This is impossible with cotton, and wool isn't much better.

There are many different kinds of functional underwear out, and increasingly, they come in a wide variety of styles and thicknesses. Look for stretchiness; the underwear shouldn't bag out. It's hard enough to skate a steep hill, and harder still when your first layer of clothing has drooped, giving you a newly lowered and suddenly restrictive inseam.

Outerwear: Given the varieties and thicknesses of transport undergarments, all you may need over them is an outer layer. Traditionally, cross-country skiers have favored non-restrictive knickers in nylon knits or wind-shedding poplin with a jacket to match. Jackets and pullovers in synthetic pile or fleece fabrics are a good bet. They have a wide temperature range and absorb little water. On all but the coldest days, you can wear a breathable but snow-shedding nylon shell lined with a light poly fleece. After an hour's skiing, the shell is usually wet, but the lining and what's under it is dry.

In recent years, droves of cross-country skiers have become devotees of Lycraetia, the goddess of Stretch and Flash. For a sport as full of dynamic, heat-producing movement as cross-country, Lycra is a natural. It came in as one-piece racing suits. But for many skiers, tights make more sense. Except for racing, fast skiers will still add a layer over their suits. So why not go with a garment that will double for running or aerobics? As for Lycra's clinging properties, it's a bit like subjecting your skiing to videotaping: you look better than you think.

Your outermost layer should be a last resort. It protects the insulation. There are many options, but basically no more than a wind shell and pants, the latter either with full size zippers or fairly long ones. Tie this layer around your waist or stuff it into a fanny pack or a rucksack. It's remarkable how quickly you'll warm up once you've cut the wind.

Feet: Cold feet is a common complain among skiers. Don't dress for skiing hours before you're on the trail, so that your socks are already soaked with sweat. And wear your ski shoes for skiing, not for breakfast. Layers are right for the feet: a poly liner sock covered with a medium-weight insulative sock in a cushiony loop terry knit. For ultimate warmth, a number of overboots are finally available. These pile-lined nylon or neoprene covers are sleek and close fitting—a far cry from the bulky models of a couple of years ago that looked like standard

Without a hat you'll take it on the chin.

issue for the Retreat from Moscow.

Hands: Gloves are necessary not only for warmth but to protect your hands from the chafing of pole straps. Make sure they are well reinforced between thumb and forefinger, or they'll quickly wear through. Unlined gloves are good for spring and will do double duty combined with a liner of transport fabric; a spare pair of liners will make the latter stages of a tour more comfortable. Nylon mitts with a synthetic pile lining work well in cold. Still, if your hands do get cold, windmill one arm at a time to push blood to your fingertips. Stay with it until your fingers tingle or until you're airborne. Just tell curious onlookers that you're winding your skating motor.

Speaking of cold hands, it is strangely necessary to turn to noses at the same time. It is not uncommon to see touring skiers take off mittens or gloves in subzero cold to extract a tissue from the inner reaches of their garments. But, once used, the tissue becomes a sodden wad in the pocket or, discarded, a ski-slowing mound in the track. Much better to resort to the St. Nick trick. Lay a finger alongside *your* nose, lean over to clear your skis, and blow through the unweighted nostril. Be assured that in the etiquette of cross-country skiing such a means of discharge is entirely proper.

Head: Your head is able to radiate up to 75 percent of the total amount of body heat lost. The old saying, "When your feet are cold, put on a hat," has lost none of its validity. A lightweight hat with a nonitch headband of transport fabric is the best choice for almost all touring. The small, neat earmuffs, used by many Scandinavians, are now widely available.

Other: A word to the gents—ladies ski on. How shall we say this? **Protect your parts!** Groinal frostnip has unfortunately been well documented in medical literature. Some of the companies that make polypropylene underwear offer special briefs with windproof nylon front panels. Lifa's version became known instantly as "fig Lifas." Lacking them, almost anything will do for a Nordic codpiece: a sock, a hat, the *New York Times*, birch bark. . . .

Remedies for wind and snow: Wind can leave your face feeling like it's been snow blasted. On downhills, you can be thankful if you're at least wearing contact lenses. Better still are the various shields that have quickly found favor. Some are just that: wraparound visors with a Velcro band that sticks to your hat. Others are oversized sunglasses, padded and ventilated against fogging. For the rest of the head, try a traditional helmet known as a balaclava, again in a transport fabric.

Spring conditions: When the world down country is mud luscious and puddle wonderful, the snowbelt, in the spring, is having some of its best skiing. It's a time to slip restraints: forget the tracks; as the snowpack corns up to the consistency of shaved ice, the woods are eminently skiable in every direction. It's a giddy time. Small wonder that our friends in California hang Hawaiian shirts next to the telemark skis in their rental racks. Still, in spite of the impulse to take it all off—or most of it—it's a time for some shrewd covering.

When we need a reminder of that, we need only check in with our associate Richard Case Sheahan. No one is more avid for vernal ventures than Casey. And no one more inventive when it comes to covering up from the sun. Mexican Mufti, Sultan of Chic—both looks have been at the 12,500-foot level on Mount Shasta, along with the requisite tape deck, lawn chairs, and sun-shunning parasol. It's easy to be deceived about how much sun you're getting, especially in high-mountain air. Sheahan suggests the obvious—a hat—but not without noting the possibilities for style. He sees utility for the long-billed fishing cap—the Gaddabout Gaddis Goes Telemarking look—but cautions about the Reverse Gabby Hayes Effect, in which an all-

Sheik and Cheeko—spring attire on Mt. Shasta

out tuck on schusses pulls the bill from its properly streamlined position over the brow and onto the face. He's also very keen on the Beau Geste look and impromptu Lawrence of Arabia head swaddlings.

Beyond such sun shields, use sunscreen—Sun Protection Factor of 15 is now a minimum, and waterproof formulas are recommended. Apply it imaginatively as sunlight is reflected off snow and can burn earlobes and armpits. Spring snow invites skiing in shorts. But a fall and slide downhill will all too readily reveal the gritty, corrosive side of corn snow. On downhills, side-zip shell pants should go on first.

CHAPTER 8

Waxing and Prepping

*T*he sight of the guy at the waxing bench, surrounded by cans, tubes, and bars of wax, irons, scrapers, and brushes, laboring as if back in the chemistry lab, gives you pause. But just ask this apparent sorcerer's apprentice, and you'll likely hear that he's having a great time. Indeed that preparing and waxing ski bases is the next best thing you can do—indoors—to being out skiing. It's no more drudgery than keeping a bike or a boat in good working order, changing the tension in the strings of a tennis racket or working on golf clubs to improve performance.

Waxing may be a little more complicated than making a peanut butter and jelly sandwich, but the aim is to keep it simple. You can pretty much do what you want, imitating the racer's iridescent combination of klisters or making use of a less flamboyant two-wax system for touring. We've seen it all on the waxing benches at ski touring centers, where "the wax of the day" is often pursued with near frenzy, yielding results that would satisfy an abstract expressionist.

Why take the time and trouble to wax well? You'll have "fast" skis that not only grip well but glide easily. Many beginning and even intermediate skiers are fearful of speed. "I don't want a fast ski," they protest. But if they think of it as doing less work, their response will be quite different.

How Wax Works

Watching good cross-country skiers, you might believe

that one wax will allow a person to ski on the flat, uphill, and down with only a slight change in technique.

How is this possible? We turn to ski scientist Mike Brady, who has long been on intimate terms with ski waxes and ski bottoms: "A waxed ski behaves this way because small microscopic irregularities of the snow surface penetrate the wax just enough to allow a good grip when a ski is weighted, yet allow a moving ski to glide." If you use wax that is too soft, the snow particles will penetrate too far into the wax and you'll be able to walk up the side of a barn door, but you'll be so sticky that you'll have to walk down the other side as well. If you put wax on that is too hard, the snow particles cannot penetrate at all. Your skis will perform like an alpine ski. They'll be like greased lightning on the downhills but in definite need of a mechanical lift on the uphills.

Grip Waxes

With the exception of alpine skiers coming to the skating side of cross-country, most skiers seem to be concerned with sorting out the ways to wax for grip for traditional kick and glide skiing. Grip waxes give you purchase on the snow. (Glide waxes, to be covered later, provide faster glide.) Grip waxes can be divided into three categories. Hard wax is for snow that is in its original condition. It may have been on the ground for several days, but it still hasn't melted, refrozen, or otherwise changed. Klister is tacky fluid, the consistency of toothpaste, for snow that has melted once, melted and refrozen, or melted, refrozen, and melted several times. After all these changes the original prickly crystals have become so rounded off that they can't penetrate hard wax; hence oozy klister.

Klister wax is halfway between hard wax and klister for use at temperatures around freezing. It's messy stuff and so seldom used that it's been dropped from one major company's line.

Ingredients: All waxes, both hard and klisters, share some common ingredients, although in different proportions depending on the type of snow for which they are intended (big wax firms no longer use beeswax, alas for the romantic legends of the past):

• Petroleum wax for water repellency.
• Synthetic rubber for adhesion.

• Oil and vaseline to soften hard wax; synthetic resin to soften klister.

We've had the curious experience of touring the catacombs of the Swix wax factory in Norway. There, in huge vats, are gallons and gallons of wax, bubbling and steaming and ready to be piped up to the cannister-filling machines. Despite a commonly held belief of skiers flummoxed by waxing, there was no eye of newt, toe of frog, wool of bat, or tongue of dog among the ingredients.

Selection: The cannisters and tubes that receive the molten wax are color-coded for easy selection. It pretty much follows the spectrum: colder colors for cold snow—green and blue; warmer colors for warmer snow—purple, red, and yellow. Since we first wrote this book, hard waxes and klisters have proliferated. No cause for anxiety. The simple fact is that the more waxes you have available, the more likely you'll have one just right for the snow conditions on a particular day. Generally, companies have added harder and softer waxes on each side of the waxes in the basic colors. You'll probably find that these waxes grip or glide better than the basics, so that touring skiers now are more comfortable with the harder and softer versions of, say, red wax, than to that venerable wax itself. Indeed, the harder red and softer blue are so useful, they're virtually basic. All told, you can ski well with a half dozen or fewer. Klisters have gotten the same treatment. The fine tuning here may be a bit much for touring skiers and best left to racers. But not to be neglected is the new universal klister, which nearly lives up to its name, and the klisters for very wet snow—just right for spring skiing.

When touring center instructors put a waxing suggestion on the blackboard, they haven't had to sacrifice a sheep or turn to a computer to get the wax of the day. They've simply checked the temperature on a thermometer located in the shade and determined whether the snow has been melted and refrozen (turning it into klister snow) and matched that with the directions on a cannister of wax. After a while you'll find that it becomes fairly routine: if the temperature is in the low twenties, red wax won't get a second glance. But humidity can make a difference. A humid day with temperatures in the twenties (Fahrenheit) might have you reaching for purple wax instead of the more obvious blue.

Many people take the posted "wax of the day" as an article of faith. One instructor friend of ours answered a telephone inquiry by saying, "Right now we're using special green." Several seconds passed, then a desperate and incredulous voice on the other end asked, "You mean it might change?" Change it may, and if you want to ski successfully you'll have to be willing to make some changes in your wax. With the wide changes of temperature in the Sierra, some days will call for a complete ransacking of the wax box; yet Alaskan skiers may cruise serenely on special green for days on end. Skiers leaving a touring center for a higher ridge may find that as the snow gets colder the higher they go, the purple wax that worked well for the first couple of kilometers has to be scraped off and replaced with blue.

Application: Most skiers, even beginners, won't have an especially hard time figuring out what wax to use. Problems occur putting the wax on the ski bottom. (One inquiring skier we overheard complaining about slippery skis was told to add a little more purple underfoot. He sat down straightaway and waxed his shoes.) Although blue may be the right wax, it will be awfully slow if applied like stucco; likewise red klister if applied thickly enough to merit anchovies and mushrooms. If in doubt, ask. Many touring center operators bewail skiers' resistance to waxing assistance cheerfully offered. "If I put on a waxing

Crayon hard wax on, then cork smooth.

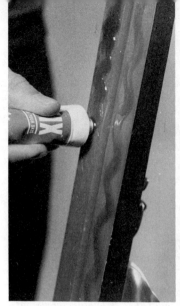

Squeeze klister on, then spread evenly.

clinic," says one of our friends, "it's a zero draw. But if I simply start waxing a ski in full view, I draw a crowd."

Hard wax is easy as long as your ski is dry (outside you may have to wipe the moisture off with a gloved hand or bandana). Peel back the wax tin and simply rub it on as if you were coloring the base with a crayon. Using the edge of the wax results in a smoother layer. Rub the wax out with short vigorous strokes of a cork (preferably a synthetic one) to make it faster and more durable. If you run your thumbnail over your ski bottom and don't roll up much wax, you haven't put enough on.

Klister is rowdy stuff and will readily transfer itself to your hands, clothes, and hair if not kept on a short leash. Warm the tube slightly with a torch, near a fire, or in your hand to make it squeezable (you don't have to bring it to a rolling boil); cold klister is impossible to extract from the tube. Squeeze a thin ribbon down each side of the groove by pressing the nozzle flat against the ski bottom. Smooth it out with the plastic spatula provided with most klisters. Or use your palm—handcleaner to follow. If you wax outside, you need a torch for spreading. If it runs over the side of the ski, you've put too much on; mop up the excess with a rag. If you're mixing klisters, dab alternate horizontal strips on each side of the groove, for an overall chevron pattern. A couple of inches between each dab should be sufficient. Apply a little heat and mix. Experienced skiers know that silver klisters have great grip on transitional snows and that they help keep other mixed-in klisters free of debris in spring snow. Again, be very sparing in putting it on and mixing it in.

Klister wax comes in a can like hard wax but behaves like klister. Daub it on in distinct intervals of a couple of inches and be prepared for the festoons of wax attaching cannister to ski bottoms even at arm's length—a bubble gum riot. Less is more here; as a matter of fact less may still be too much. Smooth it out with a torch and rag or a cork used for this wax only.

Two-wax systems: If you're just getting started in skiing or don't want to face the array of waxes and klisters (or are color blind), you can ski very nicely using the two-wax systems now on the market. They're so reliable Ned has used them on long multiweek ski expeditions. They're simple to use: one wax for dry and powdery snow below freezing and one wax for wet and packing snow above. In the Swix system, "gold wax is for cold, silver is for slop." In others, it's above and below freezing. The waxes are formulated to respond to a wide range of moisture and hardness in the snow: so even with only two waxes you get adequate performance. The secret is a subtle application of layers. Apply them thinly and cork them in well for cold dry snow. Be sparing in your first application, and if the skis are still slipping as the day warms, continue to add more wax. You get more grip not by switching to a different wax but by adding a thicker, rougher, longer coat. When the conditions get really slushy, you have to apply up to a half cannister of wet wax to get adequate grip.

A paper-thin layer of cold-snow wax, polished well with a waxing cork, works like hard green wax. A long, thick, un-polished layer of the same wax works like hard purple. A thin layer of wet-snow wax works like hard red, while a thick layer works about like red klister, but only on the flat. If you need real climbing grip in old slushy snow, you'd better use some regular red klister.

Because two-wax systems are very forgiving as snow hardness changes radically at the freezing point (the ultimately frustrating waxing temperature) and tend not to ice up as readily as regular wax, they work excellently in snow just at the freezing point and in snow lying on unfrozen ground, which is common in cities and southern areas. You can ski around Central Park in New York City, then head to Vermont or Colorado and use the same waxing system—it's adaptable. In difficult waxing conditions, even racers use it. After you become comfortable with the two-wax system you might want to try a little finer tuning by moving into the full waxing spectrum.

Wax removal and ski purification: As with walls, so with skis: the old paint has to come off before the new goes on. On a well-cared-for ski, the tips and tails gleam translucently, and in the middle of the ski there's a fine-grained blush of wax. On a neglected pair, the tips and tails are mottled and fibrous, and in the middle the wax is a thick, dirty crust. Which ski will give better glide? So keep skis clean.

Remove as much wax as possible with a scraper, working from tail to tip so that you roll up a ball of wax. If you're out on the trail, this is as much cleaning as you'll have to do. Otherwise, to prevent build-up of old waxes, scrape and then use a solvent or commercial wax remover with a rag, allowing the solvent a couple of minutes to dissolve the wax before you wipe it off. You can also use a torch to melt the wax and wipe it away, but be cautious and keep the torch moving so you don't melt the base of the ski. We recall with amusement the recent visit to Vermont of Swedish marathon coach Kjell Kratz. Looking over the wax table at one skier busily working with a torch, Kratz asked, "Why do you burn your skis?" Solvents are the safer bet.

Wax zone: To get optimum grip and glide from your waxes, put them where they'll do the most good. That means waxing the middle of the ski, leaving tips and tails for glider. The middle of the ski is the so-called wax pocket of a ski—the area of greatest stiffness, so that grip wax will have little contact with snow when you're gliding. Roughly speaking, on most higher-quality "performance" skis, it runs from the heel plate forward a foot or more in front of the binding. You can get an approximate length by squeezing skis together, while holding them up to the light and sighting along the bases. The area where there's a gap is the wax pocket. Another way to get a feel for it is to wax a long "kicker" and scrape it back, inch by inch, as you ski. At one point—the end of the wax pocket—you'll feel glide pick up without any sacrifice in grip. Scrape another inch and you might be into the wax pocket, scraping off grip.

Troubleshooting: If your skis are slippery and do not climb, your wax is too hard, you didn't put enough of it on, or what you put on has worn off. Before you make adjustments, make sure you've skied a couple hundred yards so the wax gets cooled off and skied in. (Skis should be set outside after waxing and allowed to cool.) Begin by adding a longer kicker of the same wax, especially in soft tracks filling in with snow or bush-whacking in deep snow. You may find that this "snowshear"—one softer layer sliding on a harder one—forces you to wax almost to the curve of the tip. Then go to a light application of the next warmer wax.

If your skis do not glide, you may have put on too much wax or too soft a wax, sometimes creating an instant six-inch platform of snow underfoot. Scrape and go to a colder wax.

Problems with klister usually come from putting too much on, cause it to ice up, resulting in skis that are both slow in gliding (ice in the klister) and slippery (layer of ice particles trying to penetrate iced-up klister). You can't stand around on klistered skis; put them on and start sliding. Four years ago, we suggested that touring skiers wax for the dryest snow to be encountered. Better, we said, to slip in the sunny meadow than stick in the shady forest.

Since then, there have been a couple of winters in our haunts whose prevailing conditions have called for more sophisticated waxing if skiing is to be had. And so the wax of the day has been posted as, say, "purple klister covered by purple hard wax." And virtually no one panicked! There were some questions, of course, especially from those who had been told that it's softer wax over hard, jelly over peanut butter. But for granular snow near the ski center and drier snow higher up, this combination was the best call.

How to do it? Put on a thin layer of klister and set the skis outside to freeze it. Then delicately smooth on some hard wax after softening it in the flame of a torch. Cork lightly. So, too, for hard waxes. In our area, successful waxing for early-season powder snow covering still warm ground can mean a "cushion" of special red covered with extra blue.

To prevent wax from wearing off, there are a couple of solutions. The simplest is to heat the first layer into the ski base with a torch or iron, smoothing it out with a rag, to create a good bond. Set the skis outside to cool, then cork the next layer in.

If the snow is icy and abrasive, take the time to use klister wax's even stickier cousin, binder wax. Dab it on cautiously or freeze it outside, and you'll be able to crayon it on. Smooth it out thinly with a warm iron or torch and cork; then apply a layer of hard wax, mixing it in with an iron. Set the skis outside and carefully cork in an additional layer or two of hard wax. It can't be denied that this is a little tedious. Get some help the first time. But it's worth the trouble because you will get better climb uphill and not have to stop in mid-tour to rewax. Becoming adept with binder is more important than ever, since many parks and touring centers now have sophisticated trail-grooming machinery that can render ice or crust into a very skiable—but very abrasive—granular snow. It's either binder or continued rewaxing, as downhills scour wax from your skis.

Purple and red hard waxes can get pretty gummy if crayoned on warm. Instead stroke them on gently in one direction when the wax is cold.

If you still have plenty of wax on at the end of the day's tour and snow conditions will be the same the next day, go with your old wax.

Beginners usually complain about slippery skis; for them a longer kicker of grip wax is a good idea. More expert skiers wail about slow skis; they'll want to experiment with the length, position, and thickness of the kicker and even get to know the different characteristics of the same color wax in different brands. One way to experiment is to wax each ski differently; you can always adjust the less adequate ski out on the trail.

A good wax job is worth the effort. Students who have switched skis with their instructors are usually astonished at how smoothly they glide and how little effort is needed to ski on them.

Zero-degree frustration: When snow falls at the freezing point, it occasions what is known as a "wax day." Which is not to say just that you'll use wax, but that you may use fourteen or so in various combinations. Frustration is the order of the day and madness not far off. People are not amused by an instructor who throws up his hands and says, "I don't know," to a question about the wax most suitable for this sleazy, incorrigible, wayward, coy, devilish snow.

Why? As the temperature approaches freezing, the snow decreases in hardness. Because there is less snow crystal penetration, you need a softer wax. At and around freezing, the rate of change of snow crystal hardness is so accelerated that for every tenth of a degree of temperature change, the snow hardness changes manyfold. Since no wax composition can keep up with this rate of change of snow hardness, you need many different waxes for small changes in temperature (and a lot of patience). Can there be any more practical reason to learn to skate?

Glide Waxes

You can ski quite well without paying attention to either the tips or tails of your skis, but even better if you take the time to pamper them with a little wax, thus adding performance and durability to the skis. This is vital for racing skis, but also important for touring skis, because an increasing number of them have porous or sintered polyethylene bases similar to those on the racing skis. Waxed full-length skating skis make the most of gliders.

There is no doubt that glide wax adds tremendously to your speed. This is particularly true in stiff racing skis, which ride only on the glide wax of tips and tails when going downhill. The special design of racing skis actually keeps the center gripping section up off the snow to reduce drag and increase speed.

A decade ago we used the glide wax for alpine skis. It wasn't long before special cross-country gliders, color-coded to the gripping wax, were developed. Mercifully, there are a lot fewer of them—no specials, extras, and supers. And touring skiers can simplify even further. Use one glider for conditions above freezing and another for those below. As it turns out, one wax in a company's line may have an especially wide range. The length of your glider zone is determined by the length of your kicking zone; hot wax only where you're not going to place your kicker wax. (Glide wax must be applied with heat if it is to bond with the polyethylene base.)

Just as you wax the middle of the ski according to the snow conditions for grip, so do you vary the glide wax on tips and tails for maximum glide. Racers and fast recreational skiers may change their glide wax daily; other skiers will not appreciate the performance difference enough to warrant the extra preparation time. They'll rewax only when they see whitish streaks on tips and tails, where the base has dried out.

How to put on glide wax: Place the skis on a level bench with the bases up. Heat a waxing iron with a torch or, better, use an electric iron set at "wool." Choose the appropriate glider. Press the wax against the iron, dripping a line along each side of the groove. Avoid heating the wax so much that it smokes.

Smooth out the wax by running the iron back and forth over the base. Keep the iron moving or you'll melt the plastic or cause a delamination. Reach under the ski and feel the top

Glide waxing. Drip melted wax onto ski base. If you lack a steady hand, hold tip of iron against base. Iron wax in, a couple of minutes on tips and tails.

skin. When it's warm, you've ironed enough. Allow the wax to cool.

Scrape excess wax off the base with a plastic scraper—it won't damage the bottom. Don't forget to remove excess wax from the groove with a rounded plastic item like the head of a klister spreader and to clean up drippings on the sidewall. The final result should be a base from which all wax seems to have been removed. Skiers whose glide waxings are sloppy are usually the victims of dirty waxing paraphernalia. A plastic scraper won't work well if its edge is already loaded with wax from a previous scraping. Uncleaned or uncombed brushes will leave as much wax on the base as they remove. Look to your tools!

Structuring and base prep: Glide waxing tips and tails of high-performance skis has proved to be a real advantage. But in the last six years, we realized that we were skiing not just on wax, but on a waxed *base.* And if that base were textured rather than smooth, we'd slide even more easily over the snow. Try sliding one piece of glass over another; it's even more difficult if there's a film of water between them. That could describe skiing on all but the coldest, driest snows. The effect is most pronounced on saturated, slushy spring snow.

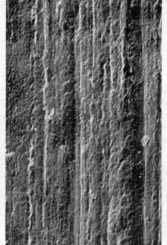

(Left to right) Micro view (100x magnification) of ski base from factory. Untreated, it will obviously be a slower ride. Ski in middle photo has been sanded with #150 grit paper, polished with Fibertex scouring pad, then waxed, scraped, and brushed. On right, the macro-structure of a rilled base (fine lines from initial prepping)

Recently, racing skis for spring conditions appeared with tips and tails microgrooved like a phonograph record to squeeze out water like the tread on a tire. Skiers also created their own structure either by taking a wire brush to striate the final layer of glider or, better, by drawing the edge of a file, tip to tail, then brushing glider out of the grooves once they'd hot waxed.

But it became increasingly clear that even on cold snow (as long as it was packed by grooming equipment), some structure in the base made for better gliding, as the tiny ridges reduced surface contact between sharp snow crystals and the base. The easiest way to do it involved sanding skis, a prospect that shocked the purists.

With the appearance of various devices to put grooves or rills into ski bases, it's become a lot faster and easier. One such riller encases the small rilling bar in a plastic housing the size of your palm. Spring-loaded plastic wings keep the riller fitting snugly over the skis' sidewalls. Press down hard with both hands and make one steady pass down the ski, tip to tail. Then buff the microscopically sharp tops of the ridges with a scouring pad—a five-minute operation. Make sure, however, that the ski is supported along its length, and that the riller will clear any vises or clamps. Then hot wax, scrape, and brush any remaining wax out of the rills, so the wax-saturated pattern can be felt if you run a fingernail across the ski. You can rill again as

(Top) Business side of rilling tool. (Center) Run riller tip to tail pressing with plenty of body weight. (Bottom) Brush hard to clean out rills. Follow with softer brush if necessary to remove all particles.

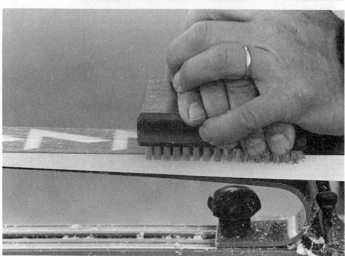

needed. Another advantage to rilling is that it displaces but does not remove base material, so you're not steadily reducing the base of your ski, as with sanding. Simple, but worth it? If you skate a lot or often ski in wet snow, it is.

Even competent skiers, who are decidedly casual about performance skiing, tell us they can feel the difference rilling makes. Some of them will even follow the racers' lead and give extra attention to prepping bases before either rilling or glide waxing. Unless you want the fastest possible ski, this isn't vital. But eliminating the high and low spots on the bases of new skis makes skis run smoother. Clean the new bases with wax remover. Then sand with No. 100-grit wet/dry (silicon carbide) paper, working tip to tail and changing paper as it loads up. A few minutes should do it. If you're not going to rill, you could follow up by sanding with No. 150-grit paper.

Sanding is also a great restorative to high-quality, sintered ski bases that have oxidized. Oxidation can occur when you store skis over the summer without first coating them with a thick and unscraped layer of glider wax. Oxidized bases have "dried out," losing some of their wax-absorbing properties. Our friends at Swix call it "plastic rust." You may hear that scraping

The frustrations of a bad wax job can call for extreme measures...

. . . while good wax makes you feel like you can tow a house.

How much of the new speed granules or powder to apply? This much. Mash carefully into base with iron to get them to adhere before ironing back and forth.

off the top layer of the base with a sharp steel scraper is best. But we don't buy it. Partly because we don't have the requisite dexterity needed to prevent gouging the base. Our friends at Swix tell us that scraping can tear the plastic bottom of the ski; there's a bite-bounce effect that can, microscopically, produce something like speed bumps. Better to sand a little.

Frontiers of glide: Skating put skiers on the fly and wax scientists back into the lab to work on new poultices that would enhance glide even more than the improvements on traditional waxes. Indeed, the new gliders are "waxes" by association rather than composition. We're not about to lecture on dry-plate solid lubrication, but we do suggest that you get to know the new waxes that answer to the two most frustrating extremes of gliding: the cold snow that feels like sand; the suction of wet snow. Cold snow is often troublesome. Swix says that your skis are slow because snow crystals are so prickly and abrasive that in a minute way, they rip open the ski base, causing drag. The new cold-snow bases are derivatives of the base material itself, and in effect, boost or armor the structure of the ski base.

Since this preparation is so hard, it will chip like the icing on a stale cupcake if you attempt to wax and scrape in the traditional way. Depending on the brand, you have to scrape when the wax is either molten or just beginning to set up. This is a two-handed, one-ski-at-a-time proposition, but worth the effort. Good glide on cold snow demands that you get all excess wax off the base. So after scraping and brushing, set skis outside to cool off; then brush again, removing wax that has "sweated" out of the base.

In between the glider and the silicon preparations for wet snow (the latter are, mercifully, applied in the accustomed manner) are graphite granulates for snow that is on either side of freezing, which partakes both of free moisture and abrasive particles—the two ends of the snow spectrum coalescing in the middle. On the ski, the combination is like a flagstone floor: hard crystals embedded in a water-repellent wax. When it comes to getting it on skis, it's strictly shake and bake, mashing what appear to be tiny ball bearings into a ski base with a warm iron. Then careful ironing and scraping and/or brushing. Undoubtedly, there's more work here. The granules tend to bounce and roll off the ski base, unless sprinkled on very carefully; the rills of a ski base will help hold them on the surface. The bottom line is, what price is that seductive free glide?

CHAPTER 9

Skiing with Elves and Elders

T he Washington's Birthday holiday has been a great watershed in the Ages of Skiing, as we see it. Our local trails swarm with kids and their parents. But when they've left, we see our trails fill with elderly skiers. That cross-country skiing seems to be growing at each end is gratifying. But still we field the same questions, season after season, from parents who find that a sunny day tour with the kids has shown them a dark side of the sport; and from seniors who wonder how—and if—to get into cross-country.

Cross-country should be great family fun, but only if you tailor the touring to the child, looking at the sport from the child's point of view. For kids, the downside of skiing with adults can be: tours that all too quickly turn into forced marches, long uphills, and constant unsolicited lessons. A better approach would be to even the split between adults and children by taking along a kid's friend, which will also hold down the pace, and parents, who are mindful of the necessity of refueling a child with hot chocolate before, during, and after.

Start kids out on easy terrain with flats, bumps, little hills, and tracks for easy sliding and striding. Don't teach too much; let them discover skiing for themselves, relying on their considerable abilities as imitators. Use plenty of games—almost anything that works on grass will work on snow: Redlight-Greenlight, tag, soccer, hockey, Foxes and Hares, relay races, Follow the Leader. And what works for American children works as well for Chinese children, some of whom skied on skis made of single pieces of walnut, as Gillette discovered in 1980 when he was a guest instructor in northeastern China. When it came to teaching *huaxue* (skiing), games solved every language problem.

157

Games will help keep it fun.

Not only do children have a short attention span, but they get tired as well. So give them a break and have some fun yourself by giving them a ride, towing your little ones uphill or along the trail by having them hold onto the handle end of your extended ski pole (for safety's sake, hold the pole above the basket and extend the handle—the blunt end—to them). They'll quickly get a sense of riding a gliding ski, of what happens when they lean forward or back. Older children can make a chain of ski poles, looping straps around baskets. Space them out so they won't ski over each other, and tow the whole bunch. Or put a child between your legs, holding onto your knees, with the little skis in the track and the big ones outside as you double-pole. Many kids like a good push at the end so they can do some free sliding.

Don't get technical. Skiing is a natural activity for children, and it's pretty likely that they aren't concerned with a lot of

"Armpit aid" turns initial security into self-sufficiency.

the hangups that adults are, like falling over, or the proper rhythm for making turns downhill (chances are it's more thrilling to bomb the slope straight, anyway).

Don't worry if your kids end up doing something besides what you had intended. As long as they're out in the snow, they're learning and discovering things for themselves. Be available to lend encouragement, but don't hover about in a heavy-handed way.

Children will discover downhills on their own and will relish falling a good deal more than you do. All you may need to do is help extract one of them from a snowbank and provide an occasional lift back up the hill, but a bit of instruction on how to get up after a fall will produce real confidence to try new things. Squatting on their skis as they move downhill will keep kids close to the snow and secure. They can push off and do some paddling with their hands, and then, in a Simon Says fashion, bob up and down until they're finally comfortable on their skis.

With very small people or ones that are not having much fun on downhills, you might try holding the child in front of you, his skis running straight as yours snowplow in a wide wedge. This way the child will glide securely and you can keep him in balance, letting go for longer periods as confidence builds. Kids won't respond very well to a lecture on how to turn, but set up a slalom course with ski poles if slalom poles aren't handy, start to snake down yourself, and watch them turn as they begin to follow you. Limbo events and a natural or constructed jump are real attractions for the close-to-the-snow crowd.

If your child is a preschooler, he or she still may be ready

Slalom courses teach coordination.

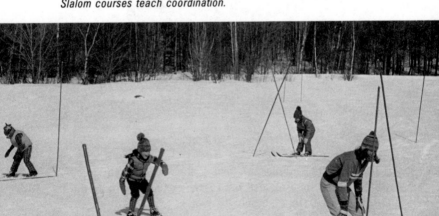

Plan your outings around the abilities of the smallest skier.

for skiing—three years old may not be too early for sliding and tumbling. If it seems to be, how about a trip on a ski-pulled sled? Remember that for little kids, skiing is only a part of winter's pleasures. You have to take a longer view—season to season—because different kids pick up skiing at different paces. Take our associates, the Jaspersohn brothers of Johnson, Vermont. Eight-year-old Andrew is an eager and accomplished skier. He can keep up with his parents on local logging roads and trails. And having worn them out he's been known to seek out his aunt and uncle, nearby, for some additional skiing. However, at age three, when he was still a sole practitioner, he liked to do some sliding—sans poles—in a well-set track. He also liked to take off his skis, jump off the trail, and roll down a hill to achieve oneness with the snow. That's all a part of the cross-country experience, and that's what his younger brother, Sam, is up to now. Sam's still working on his snowplow, still feeling better about schussing along holding his mother's hand. And just as his brother did, Sam sometimes opts for a little cross-carpet skiing indoors—a great way for a kid to become familiar with his equipment.

You don't need much of an outlay in either clothes or equipment to get kids started. Snowpants and sweaters and a jacket or vest should do it, along with extra mittens or gloves. Nor should you bundle kids up until movement is nearly impossible, but you should dress them with anticipation of plenty of time rolling in the deep stuff whether in cold Vermont or soggy Oregon.

Waxless skis are great for kids. Fit them head-high for maneuverability. Even in shorter lengths the skis will still get tangled. When this happens, lift the kid up and let his legs and skis unwind like a telephone on a knotted cord. Poles may only encumber the younger, shorter skier. But little kids should have some as well as older siblings, lest they feel left out. To get the kid skiing better—without poles—shuck yours as well. Boots for tykes now also double for winter play, while still fitting into a simple binding. Buy boots that fit now, so your child can ski with more control. Sure they'll outgrow them fast, along with the skis and poles, but with more kids skiing, the market in second-hand equipment is booming. Some communities even have a ski swap in the fall; and specialty ski shops often take outgrown equipment as trade-ins.

There's more good equipment available for kids now, and that's welcome. But until recently, no one had considered what happened when kid and equipment took to the tracks. Our friends at Idaho's Sun Valley Nordic Center suggest that adults imagine how hard it would be for them to ski with their skis two feet apart. But that's the way it is when kids ski in tracks set for

Skating's for septuagenarian Gardiner Lane.

adults. So Sun Valley has taken to setting tot-sized tracks, four inches narrower than normal. And the difference it makes in kids skiing is remarkable, they say. Grooming trails specifically for kids is catching on. But if you happen to be the groomer, skiing in your own tracks in unpacked snow, try narrowing your stride, and watch how much more easily the trailing kids ski.

The Elders. Put us in this category—in due time. Cross country's not just for the young. If we ever need reminders of the pleasures and benefits older folks can derive from cross-country skiing, we get them close to home. Gillette's mother, a former alpine skier, has skied cross-country well into her seventies, finding it a perfect exercise and a relief from walking on slippery winter roads. Dostal's father started cross-country skiing at age sixty-nine. He's now cresting eighty and still on skis.

Like many other seniors, both these parents value equipment that is, above all, stable. They both ski on the newfangled "systems" boots and bindings for more control; older skiers are just as deserving of good design in equipment as any other group of skiers. As for skis, reasonably wide for stability and waxless for convenience, thank you. Urged to try a longer ski pole, Dostal's father, no skater as yet, found that it gave him extra push in the double pole, making up for a somewhat limited range of motion, and felt more stable in striding on the flats.

If your own kids are urging you into cross-country, be mindful that their concern about your well-being could lead them to be overly-solicitous. It was a bright but cold day when Dostal got his father on skis. The younger Dostal suggested enough layers to upholster a Victorian drawing room. At the end of their tour, the well-lathered first-timer allowed as how he rather enjoyed the skiing part but could have done without the on-ski sauna.

Concern with cold is one thing. Falling's another. When Dostal's father took off on his first long solo outing, involving a climb and descent, his son was concerned that he stick to easier routes. "Don't come back down via the Haul Road and The Chute," he said.

The older skier arrived a little later than anticipated.

"You came down the Haul Road, didn't you," Dostal said. So what, he wondered, had the old man done in The Chute; could he snowplow?

"Sometimes," his father replied.

Sixtyish newspaperman Jerry Kenney likes wide stable skis. Especially when he can point them down at Crested Butte, Colorado

When that didn't work, what did he do?

"Let the skis run. Took a couple of spills."

If you're a senior, concern about falling is legitimate. But from what we've seen, the anticipation is worse than the actual tumble. And the fall itself is not as taxing as trying to get back up without the proper technique—attempting to heave yourself up only using your poles.

Still, falling on hard snow is not welcome. Both our skiing parents are fair-weather skiers. If trails are icy beyond the grooming ability of their local areas, they simply choose to ski another day. Be specific when you ask about ski conditions; ask where they've used the powdermaker. And if you're looking for mellow skiing, don't just ask what trails are "easy." Instead, be specific. Find out if a particular trail is gentle enough so that you can snowplow all the way down.

Of course, maybe you would just as soon take it in a tuck, or throw in a few parallel turns. Cross-country technique doesn't change for seniors; it's just a matter of adapting basic technique to whatever range of motion you're comfortable with.

Glide wax will still boost the traditional style.

CHAPTER 10

Racing and Training

*I*f a skier asks if you "put on bib" over the weekend, chances are you're not being queried about whether you got into some lobster. No, it's a question of whether you ski raced. If you didn't—if you haven't—we urge you to. We'll not harangue or indulge in lofty discourse on man's competitive nature. We're not zealots, just occasional racers, who have found that a half-dozen "citizen" races (ones open to all comers) give us a reason to stay in shape and add a little comic relief to the winter's skiing as racing rivalries are renewed.

Beyond the fun, there's the matter of technique. Hark to legendary hurdler Edwin Moses: "That's why you get out there and race—to find out what you're doing wrong and what you need to work on." How to get better? Put it on the line every so often.

Getting Started

To get started racing you don't have to have a lot of training, years of skiing experience, perfect technique, or top-of-the-line equipment. Just wax the skis, head to the tracks, and go for it. The racing will pretty much take care of itself if you only ski attentively. People sometimes get psyched out by the term "race." Think of it instead as a long ski in a festive carnival atmosphere with friends you may have trained or toured with and may well soon drink beer with.

Your attitude will determine what kind of a race you ski. If you're uptight or too intense, you'll not only miss the fun but have poor results. Serious enjoyment is the key to success as a

All on board—this train's going 50 kms.

citizen racer. After all, you're probably racing on a day off from work.

The menu of races to choose from in a winter is staggering. You can race at standard international and Olympic distances of five, ten, fifteen, thirty, and fifty kilometers. There's a national marathon series and one in the Midwest, where racing is so popular that one estimate has five thousand skiers at the starting line on any Saturday or Sunday. There are national and regional championships for our kind of skiers—those over thirty, masters. Kids thirteen and under can race in the Bill Koch League, named after America's Olympic medal winner and— even more impressive—World Cup Champion. The U.S. Ski Association, and its regional divisions, is the clearinghouse for most races and leagues. And if racing in the United States doesn't hold you, there's a schedule just as full in Canada, where border crossing adds a little exotica.

Along with all of this, there are other opportunities, some decidedly madcap. In our haunts in Northern Vermont, there is a race that begins on top of the local ski mountain and ends, sixteen kilometers later, in town. A bit south of us there's a ridge run. There's also a mountain ascent via a snowed-over auto road. In Crested Butte, Colorado, citizens race through back streets in the Alley Loop. In the Midwest, it's bowling league-style midweek team events under the lights. If a frantic, churning, roller-derby style is attractive, how about a mixed doubles sprint elimination competition, with head-to-head sprints of only one kilometer? The Europeans have had these leg-freshening "quickies" for years, often as a crowd-pleasing prelude to a marathon. At our local area, there's a good-humored Tuesday afternoon "fun race" that's become a real attraction for employees and lodge guests alike. It's a non-threatening, easy way into the world of ski racing.

Start small to get a feel for it. Enter a mellow five-kilometer event. If you aspire to the almost hypnotic involvement of marathons, try out the half-distance races that usually are a part of such events. The twenty-five-kilometer half-marathon will give a feeling for the full boil of mass starts, strategies carried over distance, and the finer points of feeding on the fly.

Smarts and Strategy

Whatever the race, make sure it starts when the gun goes

Racing on the exotic side: through the streets of Crested Butte, Colorado, in the Alley Loop

off and not before. Don't create a pre-event in which you spike your pulse by trying to register, get dressed, get to the bathroom, and wax the skis all in an impossibly short time. Check local weather and put glider on the night before. That's the time to check equipment as well. If you don't, you might find yourself in the sorry condition of our friend Charlie the Tennis Pro. A couple of seasons ago, he decided he'd rounded nicely into shape and wanted to go full tilt into a marathon. He opted for the sixty-five-kilometer Mont Ste. Anne Loppet in Quebec, one of Canada's best races. He was still adjusting his poles at the start, and lost both in the crunch. At twenty-five kilometers, he skied off the trail to relieve himself, only to discover that the fly front on his borrowed one-piece suit didn't match up with the neck zipper on the polypropylene union suit underneath. Then at thirty kilometers, his bindings, which had loosened up the week before, pulled out of his skis. "I've done it all," he said. "For me the race is over." Details, details.

If there's time, check out the more radical sections of the course: corkscrewing downhills, grain elevator uphills, the sudden skate turn. If you have no familiarity with the course, at least check a profile map. Try to relate the climbs and descents to what you know from your local area, so that if the map indicates a climb of two hundred feet in three kilometers, you'll know how much exertion to anticipate.

Many citizen races—and all marathons—are mass-start affairs. If you find yourself skiing alone, you are either (a) exceptionally fast, (b) extraordinarily slow, or (c) have taken a wrong turn and are now the sole entrant in an orienteering event. Buffetings, logjams, and entanglements are inherent in mass-start races, and all the more so because of the lateral scissoring of skating. How to protect yourself in the maelstrom? First, stake out your territory in the starting line, placing your poles to the side to discourage encroachers. Station yourself in the pack according to your ability; if you're not a hotshot, you don't want to be engulfed from the rear. Race courses usually begin on an open field and narrow as they get into the woods. Getting to the outside may give you more room to work.

Technically speaking, almost anything goes. Double poling from the start, especially in a skating race, is stable and a good way to avoid getting tripped up; indeed some races will have a "no skate zone" for the first two hundred meters. Don't let yourself be pushed around, pulled down, or skewered. Be

A mass start puts a premium on staying upright.

prepared to go hard enough in the beginning until the masses sort themselves out, and less frantic rhythms are established. This will be easier if you've warmed up properly. Begin as much as an hour before the start with easy skiing. Include what coach Dick Taylor calls a little "crisp skiing." Then ski easily just before getting to the line, to stay warm and loose.

Keeping up a good rhythm will ensure a good race. Most citizen racers cannot go all out for even ten kilometers. So be clever. Think about the most economical way to ski a section of the course. Can you cruise behind another skier, letting his rhythm smooth out your own? Look for cost-free places to make your move and pass another skier. Why pass on an uphill? It's taxing, and there's often little room. Remember that your body has a thirty-second lag time before experiencing the effects of a hard hill. And if you're laboring at the top, you might well compromise your efforts on the following flat or downhill.

Not all the bumps and dips are in the terrain you're racing on. In a race of any length, there are bound to be some highs and lows in your mind as well. In a long race, you'll go through stages of thinking you can't ski on. You may feel like an Escapee from a Chain Gang, who's picking up the ball and chain and dragging it another kilometer, only to drop it again at the top of a hill. But your body will go farther than you think, and you'll experience the euphoria that is common to long-distance races.

Still, if your entry fee seems at some point to have bought an unwelcome Out of Body Experience, it may be because you're not feeding properly. If you're active enough to ski race, your diet probably is weighted in favor of carbohydrates, and you've taken on more before the race. Being hydrated is most important, too. Our associate Rob Sleamaker in Burlington, Vermont, an exercise physiologist who has worked extensively with U.S. Biathlon Team members, reminds us that losing fluids invariably means a loss in performance. There can be as much as a 10- to 15-percent drop in fluids in a marathon. While you can't replace all the fluid you lose during a race, you can rely on the water you've taken in the day before, as well as just before the race.

Then too, you must drink or "feed" during the race. Race organizers usually have feeding stations every five kilometers. Take the time to slow down so that the liquid goes in your mouth rather than down your suit. Don't neglect the first couple of stations because you're feeling strong; you'll pay for it later. Despite well-meaning efforts of volunteers, feeding stations aren't always what they should be. Offerings of solid food won't help during a race. (One friend was once presented with prime rib thirty-five kilometers into a marathon.) And energy-replacement drinks favored by many athletes sometimes haven't been diluted enough. The solution, if you will, is to carry one of the neat waist packs resembling a foam can holder on a web belt. It accommodates the standard or oversize plastic bottles found on bicycles, and offers the opportunity for quick-draw replenishment with the fluid of your choice when you want it.

Training

You don't have to be a student of sports science to agree that you'll race better in February if you've done some training in September or earlier and continued it right through the winter. We won't presume to offer a prescriptive "training menu," broken down week by week. If you're serious, that's necessary; but the best resort is a sports physiologist like our associate Sleamaker, whose Compufit process creates a personalized training program, or one of the numerous off-season clinics put on by the U.S. Ski Association. Of course, you don't

We're partial to training on water. The authors at cross purposes from the start, Cape Cod

have to have racing aspirations: the off-season activities we suggest should help anyone's track skiing or touring.

Chances are that if you're getting into even occasional racing, you already have an active lifestyle that carries right through the snowless off-season and are doing things that have some carry-over to skiing. You're probably a runner or cyclist. You get in some long hikes on summer weekends. We like to get on the water; Dostal opts for a racing canoe, Gillette for a rowing shell. (As messy about training as ever, Gillette recently rowed from South America to Antarctica.)

It's not just that these pursuits help you to keep up a general level of fitness from which you can build in the winter. They may also be ski-specific—or can be made so—to better simulate the movements of skiing and work the muscles that will be heavily recruited once you're on the snow. Paddling, for example, not only simulates the "high hand" of skating, but pressing the paddle into the water and steadily building pressure, rather than slamming it in, is just the way you would use your ski pole. Vigorous uphill hiking, driving the foot forward and extending the rear foot, coupled with an aggressive arm swing is a better approximation of the demands you'll put on muscles when you ski. Add your poles, and the effect will be even better. Not only will you strengthen your arms but, with a little coaching from a friend, you can eliminate technical errors as well, such as levering your elbow back instead of driving your hand down and past your hip. You can even duck walk your way

Tatooing's optional, but hiking with ski poles is a training basic.

uphill, simulating skating, or do a little bounding to build leg strength.

You'll see an increasing number of people (and virtually all serious skiers) on roller skis and roller skates with four in-line wheels, now generically known as "blades." They're not for everybody. Traffic-free roads with good pavement are vital. And while these rollers are cheaper than skis (about $160 and up), they require more maintenance as tires and bearings wear. Many coaches regard blades as less ski-specific than roller skis. And they invite some bad habits. But they turn readily and are great fun (just don't try to diagonal stride). Roller skis used to be three-wheelers, ratcheted so you could kick and glide in a diagonal stride. But with the surge of skating, most roller skis are now two-wheelers with barrel-shaped tires that can roll over, simulating the edging of a skating ski. Some have a ratcheted wheel for striding. However, you may find that the two-wheelers are a bit unstable for secure, technically correct striding. Replace ski pole baskets with a plastic ferrule, housing a sharp carbide tip. It's vital to keep them sharp; an inexpensive diamond particle sharpener works well, especially in a coarse grit.

Summer or winter, there's only a certain amount of time for training. Sleamaker suggests using it wisely—a departure for many skiers. Citizen racers often accumulate hours of what he calls "junk intensity." That is, they train in a narrow heart-rate zone. It's not slow enough to build a good endurance base and refresh the body for fast skiing. And it isn't fast enough to get the body accustomed to a racing pace. Instead they are training in between, beating themselves up. Sleamaker suggests only a couple of hard days a week. Otherwise, you should be skiing at a pace that is so easy as to be "guilt producing." If you have to walk the hills to keep your heart rate down on an easy day, do so. On hard days, he suggests a good warm-up followed by short intervals of one to five minutes of skiing at a heart rate about five beats below your race pace, to get used to the physiological changes of racing—the hard breathing, throbbing in the head and tingling in the legs. But avoid hard intervals right before a race.

You need a plan, Sleamaker believes, and you need to stick to it. Elite skiers might train twenty hours a week, racing forty times a winter. If you can spare only six hours a week for training, get the most out of them. But don't be a slave to it, forcing yourself into a hard workout despite signs of protest from your body. In this regard, some of the best advice we've heard comes from former U.S. Ski Team coaching staff member Dick Taylor: "Be generous with yourself."

Dryland training on roller skis

CHAPTER 11

Cold-weather Smarts

You and two friends are eight miles from the car, night is falling, it is snowing. The gentle atmosphere you were enjoying on the trail turns threatening. The snow, slippery pavement underfoot normally, may soon have to serve as an improvised home. The weight of accessories in the small pack you've been toting, and resenting, is now welcome. Your recall, if not precise in remembering landmarks you passed on the way out, certainly is precise in picturing the head lamp nestled on the dash of the car. You left it behind because, "it's only a short jaunt." You now have the unsettling suspicion that you're about to become part of a Jack London story.

If you ski a lifetime, chances are you'll play at least a bit part in such an adventure. In his early days, soon after he went west to see what the big mountains offered, Gillette had such an experience. With his friends, Jeff and Donna, Gillette decided to ski the twenty-five miles from Yosemite Valley to Tuolumne Meadows (nine thousand feet) to do some winter climbing. They wanted to do it in one day; some feat in those early days of cross-country skiing. The accomplishment was very important, and, after a dawn start, drew them on through heavy Sierra snow.

At Tenya Lake, they took inventory and came up with one quart of water for the three of them. Phrases like, "I thought you were carrying a full jug," were bantered about. Halt, start the stove, melt snow? No way. Water consumption took a backseat to time consumption. "One day or bust," they laughed. They continued on with the sweaty race. Their backpacks seemed weightier as the hours wore on.

Arctic cold even in California

The sun hit the horizon about the same time the team began to hit the wall. Four miles to go. Only four. Bivouac? "There's a cabin for us in Tuolumne." Change of socks? "Time's a-ticking. Gotta go." Four hours later, at 9 P.M., the four easy miles were behind the now tottering, dazed skiers. Not slackers or complainers, none of them rested nor spoke. Jeff should have, earlier. He waited until the end of the marathon, then announced, "I can't feel my feet."

Finally inside the cabin, which had seemed so critical to win, Jeff displayed his wood-hard, waxy white digits of podiatry. Stove-heated lukewarm water, accompanied by bite-the-bullet pain, thawed both feet out. The next day the park service carried him out.

That happened to Gillette a hundred experiential years ago. Since, he's skied the backcountry hundreds of times with hundreds of partners. He's seen everything that can break or bruise do so.

Backcountry Skills

You need more than a good set of legs for the backcountry. You need know-how. The acknowledged expert in the backcountry is much more than the purveyor of pretty turns. He's the guy—or she's the gal—with the spare pole basket to re-

Cause for celebration: another night of cheating the cold

place yours, the needle and dental floss to fix a ripped-out pack strap, the right screwdriver to remount an itinerant binding. He's the guy that remembers outgoing landmarks during the incoming darkness. He exudes confidence, because he's spent the necessary years to get it right: not just the technique, but the orienteering, mountaineering, and winter backpacking. He has the experience to know when the terrain ahead is too much. Long after you've got your "teles" down pat, stick with these crafty guides until you've got it right yourself. In the end you want to be self-reliant, confident, and able to cope in the wilderness.

Face it, trouble happens in the backcountry. It is winter: you lose light early, equipment breaks, people break. Cool improvisation will see you through. Know the snow conditions. In the East, the trail is not always the same from one day to the next; packed powder can turn into rain crust overnight. Different snow can shoot the difficulty rating out of sight and beyond your ability to cope.

You don't have to go on big trips in big mountains to take the proper precautions or to get into trouble. Daily trail sweeps at touring centers often disclose ill-prepared skiers, who are lost or overly fatigued even on well-marked trails. The result is usually acute discomfort. But farther out, on unpatrolled wilderness trails on a cold January night or rainy March afternoon, the stakes are higher.

You can't eliminate risk in skiing off-trail, but you can reduce it to manageable levels. Even if you're on a marked trail system, when the lights go out, you're suddenly in the backcountry, like it or not. No longer are there visible signs to show the way. It's now time to have at least some basic outdoor skills and planning.

Safety in numbers: Four is the ideal number for a touring party. Decisions are fast, camaraderie close, impact minimal. Expectations for the outing are easy to collate; it's hard to combine tourers who want to photograph leisurely with skiers who want to make a horse race of the day.

Four is also the perfect number to deal with injuries. At the end of a long tour, lugging yourself the last few miles can seem like the final miles of a marathon run. But this is nothing compared to the labor of evacuating an injured skier. The best strategy for the injured is to administer first aid, make the person comfortable, leave the injured party with someone in atten-

Even in sunshine, extra clothing goes on when the skis come off.

dance, and ski with a partner for help. If you have to evacuate, build a sled using the injured's own skis and poles. Lash the poles in an X-shaped pattern to the skis. Extra branches lashed on reinforce the toboggan. Take it from us, the ensuing haul is as unpleasant as it sounds.

Leadership is also important. Gillette likes leaders who give the impression of ruling by democracy, but who, in truth, rule by benign autocracy.

Equipment: Carefully inventory your personal possessions and analyze how each might help you. Socks don't always go on the feet in a situation like this—they're good mitts as well. Consider using shoestring or belts for rope, skis and poles for building shelter, backpack to stuff your feet into, shoes to sit on, ski tip as a shovel, ski tail to cut snow blocks, ace bandages from a first-aid kit to keep head, feet, or hands warm, and tape as string.

If you've planned ahead, a light pack with some things that could prove indispensable during an all-day (all-night?) tour are: extra food and water, a windbreaker, a jacket, extra socks and mitts and hat, sunglasses, sunscreen, extra wax, scraper, matches, map, compass, headlamp, a simple first-aid kit, and a repair kit.

When you head to the high country, you'll want to add a foam pad, a stiff plastic shovel, an avalanche beacon, an avalanche cord, and a probe pole. Include snow pit analysis aids, such as a hand-held magnifying lens, a snow thermometer, a stiff card, a notebook, and a snow crystal identification chart.

Repairs: A few things can have a chilling effect on an out-of-track tour, and broken equipment is one of them. The last-minute checks should be exhaustive. Are the baskets on the poles split or cracked? What about the boots? Are the pin-holes and toes intact? But no matter the precautions, stuff still breaks.

Adjust clothing according to your body's thermometer—and pack so you don't have to excavate.

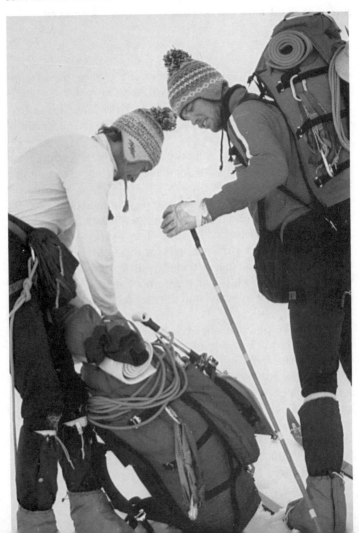

What can you do? A pretty solid repair job, actually, if you take along the right items and the proper improvisational spirit. Rummage through an experienced skier's repair kit and this is what you'll find: ski and pole splints; a spare pair of bindings; baskets; golf tees to fill up binding holes if screws work loose; a couple of full tubes of epoxy; C clamps; vise grips; a posi-driver screwdriver; wire (a makeshift cable binding, among other things); and either strapping or duct tape. The right items in a repair kit can work on most anything in need of surgery, including an edged telemark ski that might have broken in two. Such a ski, properly field repaired, can hold up to four days of hard skiing, as well as the necessary exit from the backcountry.

Ski and pole splints are vital items. Pole splints are simple: a split metal sleeve (even a recycled beer can will do) tightened down with three hose clamps. Components are readily available. The ski splint is a ski scraper, like the one commonly used to flatten out ski bases. Have a machine shop punch out screw holes on the splint, in vertical and horizontal patterns.

Then if a ski breaks, say, in its forebody, load up the broken innards with epoxy, pulling back the ski's top sheet a bit if necessary. Use ski splints top and bottom, binding them with a small C clamp and a six-inch pair of locking vise grip pliers. When the epoxy hardens, take apart the sandwich and screw one of the splints to the top of the ski, starting the holes with the awl of your pocketknife. It's important to realize that this procedure is effective on skis with full steel edges, not cracked or partial ones, as the full edge gives the necessary structural integrity.

But a steel-edged ski isn't needed for a lot of out-of-track touring. If an edgeless ski breaks outside the tip area, cut away the shorter part and remount the binding forward, so that your heel is still on the ski. Progress may be reduced to a hobble, but some progress is better than none at all.

With a plastic ski, edged or not, however, it's rare to break a tip, as so often happened to the old woodies. Indeed, we usually don't even include a spare tip in our kit. Should one break, tape the tip under the forebody of the ski, so that it overlaps slightly.

Let's return to your emergency night in the open. The snow is falling hard enough to blot out your tracks.

Digging in: First, assess your predicament by consulting your topographical map. (You did bring one, yes?) By recording landmarks while outbound, there's a good chance you can backtrack. This is usually the fastest way out and the best option. Roads and power lines that run parallel to your route may be easily located by sharply angling your direction. In settled parts of the country, heading downhill may lead you to a road, but out West downgrades may lead you to dead ends.

Sometimes it takes more courage to stop and bivouac than to force march onward. Trouble compounds with each additional step taken into the night or into white-out conditions, where you're almost certain to lose your bearings.

Whether in the East or the West, try to retreat to the trees. Nestle into a tree well (evergreens umbrella nicely). Tie a strip of bright cloth to a tree so searchers can find you. Make a bed or seat of boughs to keep you up off the snow. Build a fire. (Be resourceful: medical gauze stuffed into a cannister of hard ski wax becomes a candle for starting fires.) Incidentally, for this you need matches. If you've forgotten them, or they're not waterproof, you'll have plenty of time during the cold hours ahead to contemplate your oversight.

A couple, benighted on the trail, returned two pairs of nicely roasted and charred rental skis, along with melted boots, to the Yosemite Mountaineering School. Although they had built a fire from available forest wood, they confessed to adding their skis from time to time. Normally it's not such a hot idea to

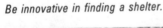

Be innovative in finding a shelter.

Close but warm in a snow cave

burn your means of transportation. Fortunately they left enough of the skis intact so they could ski out the next morning.

Above timberline in the West, scour out a hole in a stable slope and crawl in, or dig a snow cave. Snow is a darned good insulator. You can be safe and even comfortable in a snow cave. Tie your locator strip of bright cloth to a ski stuck upright. Hunker down out of the wind. Put on extra clothing as soon as you stop working, especially dry socks and a dry layer next to your skin. (This may entail exchanging the first and second layers.) Put on your outer wind-protection layer. Create a bed or sitting platform from your backpack, rope, or small foam pad (if you came prepared). All this cuts heat loss. Stay calm, assured that plenty of people have made it through a night out. Entertain yourself—compose an ode to your pj's neatly folded at home.

Staying dry and stoked: Success, whether you're traveling or bivouacing, depends on how dry you stay. Stay dry and your confidence will stay buoyed, and your decisions will stay sharp. Soggy skiers are not known for their good judgment.

Water can assume any number of guises to harass you. It's always freezing or thawing or vaporizing, conniving in new ways to sodden your clothing. How do you get a case of the damps? The most common is overexertion while maintaining too fast a pace or pushing an enduro trail-breaking session, and thus working up a sweaty lather. The expression, "You're really steaming along," may not be a compliment while you're on a full-day tour. Save the saunas for home where you can towel off. Or, if you've got to hit it hard, at least pare down the layers so rivers aren't running down your breast bone.

More ways to wet yourself: eggbeaters are a tried and true method. So, if you're prone to auger in on downhill runs, don

Streams: The crossing can be worse than the anticipation.

Constant reclining in this posture will eventually take a toll on comfort, at least

your windbreaker prior to take-off. There are yet other water hazards lying await. Snow bridges spanning streams are the easiest way to get to the other side, but they're also the easiest way to sample hip-wading techniques out of legal fishing season. Check things out before barreling in. On a long tour, consider the future consequences of a present action—it may catch you later. Don't be a killjoy, just keep the snowball fights to short skirmishes.

You burn a lot of calories during a cold day on the trail. Re-stoking keeps you warm, on the go, and in a bright mood. Instead of stopping once to gorge lunch, snack every hour or so, and pour some liquid in. Dehydration pulls down your performance, as well as your ability to acclimatize if you're at any kind of altitude. (Climbing in the Himalaya, we drank four quarts each day.) With a bent toward steamy stuff, we like the luxury of carrying a thermos on some tours when the mercury has dropped.

Carrying things one step further, add extra rations as you add extra days to your tour. Extra is the key here. If you have a

four-day itinerary, pack at least five days of food so you can wait
out bad weather.

Pacing yourself: Unlike our chapters on technique,
where you'll find plenty of advice on how to move it along the
trail and click off those kilometers, here we're talking more
about stop action. We recommend a good stop now and again.
There's a reason for stopping, and a method of stopping. Stop
to re-layer or un-layer, stop to eat and drink, stop to turn back
while there's still plenty of daylight. Heck, stop just to look
around. Sometimes stopping is the hardest thing to do, when
you are motivated toward fitness or reaching trail's end. But it
pays off. (And it's a legitimate excuse to be lazy, momentarily.)

Hypothermia: Skiers who lather themselves and refreeze
are headed for trouble. Doctors have a term for the slow freeze:
hypothermia. The skier shivering at the end of the day in soaked
blue jeans and thin wet gloves is at risk. If that skier is within
easy distance of a touring center or farmhouse, it is not as dangerous as if he had to pass the night in a tent. Dostal once skied
across the Sierra with two out-of-shape skiers who over-
extended the first day and were so hypothermic that they
couldn't understand simple directions on how to help put up a
tent. The wind wasn't blowing, they weren't wet, but they had
simply burned all their fuel and gotten cold quickly.

Prolonged exposure to cold (not necessarily below freezing) and wind and wet can cause a lowering of the temperature
of the body core. Heat loss exceeds heat production. If the body
temperature falls below a certain point (about ninety-two degrees Fahrenheit), the process is irreversible. Symptoms vary,
but the most common are intense shivering, fatigue, numbness,
poor coordination, impaired speech, weak pulse, blue lips, and
irrational thought.

Treat the victim by preventing further loss of body heat,
then adding warmth. This means you must find shelter, replace
wet clothing with dry and add layers of insulation, get the victim
into a prewarmed sleeping bag, build a fire, surround him with
warm bodies, and get him into a hot bath if possible. Curiously
enough, avoid giving hot drinks to cure acute cases. The body
reacts by opening the constricted vessels carrying cold blood in
the arms and legs. This flood of frigidity into the body core can
be critical.

Over time, with many backcountry miles under your skis,
you'll develop judgment and instinctive surveillance from skiing

Mt. McKinley, Alaska

with good guides. It's a self-reliant awareness and level-headed competency that you're after. No longer will the challenge of getting from here to there over that ridge seem so intimidating. You'll know the techniques of moving and stopping. Survival strategies, not an end unto themselves, give a certain refreshing freedom on the snow.

Avalanches: Snow lying on level ground is a dormant blanket. Snow lying on an incline is altogether different; it is alive due to the tug of gravity. Add too much weight on it, pump too much water in it, or inject a split personality through it and, like a person with the same afflictions, there's unpredictability. Overweight, drunk, schizophrenic snow acts by no consistent formula. At different times it's playful, moody, troublesome, confused, or very dangerous. It's always unpredictable.

That's the personality of the substance on which you ski. Normally, you, the skier, are the moving object. When the tables are reversed, and the snow starts moving, there's trouble. The

Avalanches are best appreciated at a distance.

trick is to stay out of moving snow.

Avalanche prediction is, at best, an inexact science. For every rule there is an exception; experts speak of probabilities rather than certainties. There's an aura of shamanism to the science; but it's the only way to calculate which hillsides are safe to ski, and which are on a hair trigger.

There are scientists who have devoted lifetimes to studying avalanches. So why is the science still so uncertain? The answer is the variables involved: the infinitely different forms that snow can assume on a limitless number of slopes under constantly changing systems of weather. Plus, water throughout the snowpack is always assuming new guises: melting, percolating, lubricating, sublimating, and recrystalizing. In spite of these difficulties, every year some of the black magic of prediction is replaced by conclusions you can stand by—or ski under.

How does this affect you as a skier? If you ski above or beyond the forest, you must assess snow safety. Many skiers who ski the backcountry think they know a good deal about avalanches on the basis of accumulated experience. That gives them an intuitive basis of judgment, enough to say, "This slope feels safe today." They've developed a suspicious sense of snow-laden slopes and have learned to listen to warnings such as windslab settling underfoot. But do they really know? Most skiers of this ilk have few hard facts by which to back up their conclusions in this potentially life-and-death game.

Formal training under the tutelage of recognized experts is the best way to learn. Courses are offered through many of the larger ski-touring centers and mountaineering shops. Make sure you choose a seminar that is taught mostly on snow in the field. Here you'll have a chance to dig a snow pit and examine, with a hand lens, the different layers that make up the snowpack. And you'll practice using avalanche transceivers to search for and locate buried victims.

As you talk with those in the know, you realize two things. First, insignificance counts. The key element in a snowpack that can spell disaster may be a wafer-thin feature hidden far below the surface. Seven-week-old rain crust, no more than an eighth-of-an-inch thick and buried three feet down, can trigger an entire slope. Or an equally thin layer of depth hoar can be the trigger. A snow pit will reveal these. You also may be able to predict these potential triggers by keeping a record of the weather and snow cycles. The key to determining slope stability

Research the snowpack before you let them run.

in mid-February may be something that occurred in December.

Second, the experts are terribly cautious. They have had too many narrow escapes. Many simply don't ski steep back-country terrain during midwinter months, even though the powder is most splendid then. They delay until spring when corn snow is stable. Even in spring, those in the know carry trans-ceivers, shovels, probes, and a snowpack analysis kit. And they take the time to dig a pit and examine the layers. If there is any doubt about stability, they adjust. Nobody is afraid to say no. There is always a slope of another exposure to ski, or, if every-thing seems weird, there is always another day.

Here are a few more points to bear in mind. The best slopes for skiing in the backcountry are usually those that pre-sent the most deadly slide danger: open bowls and couloirs twenty-five- to forty-five-degrees steep. High avalanche danger results from storms with snow falling more than an inch an hour or accumulating more than twelve-inches total or with winds in excess of twenty miles an hour. Also bad are storms starting with low temperatures and dry snow followed by wetter, heavier snow that produces a poor bond. Leeward slopes and

cornices tend to be unstable. Slab avalanches cause most acci-
dents. Usually avalanches that eat people are triggered by the
skiers themselves.

Eighty percent of avalanches occur during or just after a
storm. Patience pays off. In New Zealand, during Gillette's
traverse of the Southern Alps, his party once waited three days
after a heavy snowfall (even though they were low on food) before skiing through a narrow valley threatened by multiple slide
paths.

Observation pays off. Gillette and two friends made the
first nordic descent of the steep north face of Anniversary Peak
in Canada's Bugaboo Mountains. From a cabin across the valley, they watched the mountainside for twelve days. During that
time they skied other slopes. When they felt they knew the char-
acter of the run, and the snow seemed right, they climbed to the
top. They spent an hour digging a pit and assessing the pack. It
was stable. They skied one at a time so only one would be exposed to danger, and stopped at islands of safety (clumps of
trees or rocks) for protection should the slope let go. It was an
ecstatic ending to two weeks of powder hounding in North
America's ski-mountaineering mecca.

CHAPTER 12

Backcountry Skiing

*B*ackcountry skiing begins when you jump out of prepared tracks and leave signature snow on a path of your own making. It's a jump, or at least a step out, into terrain that offers the possibility of adventure and demands the fine art of improvisation. It's a refreshing tonic, a change of venue, a different playground. Getting off the trail is for everybody, because it embraces everything in skiing. It's complete skiing as skiing was originally, where you mix nordic and alpine, skating and diagonal, telemark and slalom, beginner and expert maneuvers. It's where you mix technique and tactics.

How many times have you skied the tracks at your local ski area? How many times have you cavorted in the trees and in unbroken snow to one side of them? We're not talking headwalls or cold sweat, just a change for the better. Jump. Shake yourself loose. After relentless track training, it's not unusual for racers to get itchy and spring into the trees and fire off a couple of tellies in space available. Indeed, it's healthy. You too. Follow your property line; ski the fields and hills beyond town; follow the animal tracks; moonlight; bushwhack the tight trees of the East and spring off a snow-capped stump; descend a couloir in the Sierra; telemark a Rocky Mountain bowl; ski hut to hut—Aspen to Vail; explore the Ruth Amphitheater beneath Mount McKinley; challenge the European Haute Route; swing down from the summit of a Himalayan peak. Heck, why stop? Join the Ski Club of Uganda by skiing the snowfields of the equatorial Ruwenzori Mountains. Gillette did, and you can be the next card-carrying member. Enlist now.

Gillette's early skiing focused on down-track racing for

Backcountry skiing—always a refresher

Backcountry no farther away than your backyard

ten years. Then he churned through fifteen years of western ski mountaineering and international expeditions before he found out about IT. Returning to Vermont, he found a whole new world of off-track skiing in his own backyard. He set upon it with an enthusiastic abandon.

Once he and some friends traversed the exposed crest of New Hampshire's Presidential Range, all in one day. At dusk, as they started the final descent down Crawford Path, a steep,

Even on skis, be a bender of birches.

sliver-thin, tree-banked hiking trail, everyone was beat and spiritless and dreading the epic exit ahead. It turned out to be a run of their lives. Snowshoers had packed a runnel down the center of the trail; soft snow lay eighteen inches deep on the sides. Someone took the first spontaneous schuss, and the game was on.

Practiced technique? Who needed it. They were gravity-squirted, like a watermelon seed pinched between fingertips. Airborne with no landing rights. Eyes watering, they zipped down the slot like bobsledders, crouching low, cornering like pursued dwarfs, skimming trees. Ever faster until they HAD to pull out. Jumped up, turned skis ninety degrees, cratered into cushy snow. Repeated until sidelined by silliness. It was no technique Gillette had ever used before, but it worked.

Bag your reverence. There's no one right way to ski the backcountry. Improvise according to how you feel, and what the snow and lay of the land demand. To discover the fun and challenge, sometimes you need skiing techniques that transcend ski discipline.

Such snow may be only a step off machine-set track.

Get your backcountry legs on day tours.

If it's quality you're after, go back to the country. There are a zillion skiers nowadays. Many prepared cross-country trails are loaded with skiers tip to tail, most ski area slopes are knee to elbow. In contrast, the backcountry lies pristine after each fresh snowfall—and it's free for the taking. Outflank the competition. Go back. Your effort to get to the backcountry—whether it be a step away or miles away—will be repaid many times in the quality of skiing. There, high and open untouched slopes give way to rhythmical slalom glades in the forest that, in turn, give way to undulating fields over which to kick and glide toward home.

You don't have to know much of anything special to exit from the marked trails at ski touring centers and experiment close to the ski freeways. You only have to be in a state of mind that allows you to be a little more adventurous toward winter. If you ski with wilderness-smart people and pick your route carefully, going farther afield on a day tour doesn't require you to be a technical expert or a yeti. Basic skills such as traversing, sidestepping, and sideslipping will allow you to enjoy out-of-track travel to wonderfully different places that once seemed out of reach. You can build up your experience by taking progressively bigger bites out away from the groomed trails.

Start by doing day tours or just hour-long stints off marked trails. Many touring centers have trails that are ungroomed and unpatrolled. Day tours are the best because they aim for the most exquisite skiing. They allow you to choose the weather and snow conditions you prefer, whereas during multiday treks you are often forced to travel in storms or unruly snow, which raises the level of commitment and potential for error. Plan your itinerary so the length of the tour can be easily shortened if necessary, and consider following unplowed roads to insure gradual grades and foolproof navigation. Day tours present less risk by staying closer to civilization. Finally, the small, light-weight packs used on day tours give more freedom of movement than those required for long trips. Short jaunts allow you to play and try new things.

The fun of a day tour is sometimes submerged under the sweaty work of busting trail upward. Be clever. Consider driving to the top of a pass served by road, maybe shuttling autos for more runs. Or ride the lifts at a commercial alpine area and ski out onto undeveloped terrain from the summit terminal. Make certain you check with the ski patrol on the policy of skiing out-of-bounds. Check on that day's avalanche danger: when there is no danger of avalanche, most western ski areas open the backcountry served by their lifts. Or consider traveling the tracks of touring centers to move quickly to the backcountry. But as you

Norwegian Alps

Eve Icefall, New Zealand Alps

probe farther out, you enter country that can bite back. Then you need to be crafty in reading terrain and snow, you need to have wilderness skills, you need to rely on your own judgment, you need to have confidence in your companions, and you need some solid skills to handle challenging ups and downs in all kinds of snow.

There's a lot of help available to make it easier to get started. There is equipment specifically designed for back-country versatility. Choose it for the terrain you'll be skiing and look for durability and versatility. (We're more specific in the chapter on equipment.) Since there are no lifts in the back-country, uphill and downhill are part of the same sport. Back-country skiers often want one set of equipment that will perform with style and safety on classic ski tours, at alpine ski areas, and on a first descent in the high peaks. Today's high-tech gear allows you to mix alpine and nordic techniques, combining downhill control and speedy excitement with free-heeled mile-age cross-country.

There's more. You don't have to lug a fifty-pound pack and hunch in a snow cave to do a backcountry trip. There are accessible alternatives. In the western mountains, huts and yurts are snug destinations. In the East, you can ski inn to inn, eating gourmet meals all the way.

How do you get better at backwoods skiing? You could follow the advice of one accomplished veteran: "Ski the worst snow you can find until you can't stand up anymore." This is, if you will, the Emersonian approach; one that may well work, but one that will just as surely put stress on equipment, physique, and patience.

A course or two on wilderness skiing or some one-on-one tutoring on closely supervised day tours may be a more attractive and effective option. Depending on where you're skiing, it's probably a safer one, too. There are always things to learn about staying comfortable in the snow, moving more gracefully, observing and interpreting more accurately. Even though they're limited, the schools that offer structured backcountry-skills programs—be they winter camping seminars, avalanche safety courses, or telemark instruction—can be found in most parts of the country where mountains meet snow.

So now you know the ancestry of those merrily un-manicured snow signatures beyond the marked trails; a skier has been unabashedly bitten by his pioneering heritage. A perfectly professional instructor has genuflected onto powder on a wide curve off the machine-set tracks and returned to kick and

Track-setting, backcountry style

Backcountry autograph party

glide, leaving a single, skinny telly track of spontaneous inspiration. The sport is changing. Track skiers are out in the woods and bowls where uniqueness spells quality. Here, every vertical foot to swoosh down is valued, not to be squandered as at a commercial lift area. Off-trail skiing somehow develops a camaraderie of working with friends, not outdoing them, and a goofy kind of fun as you solve the unexpected problems of cranky snows or tight-treed gullies or a forgotten corkscrew for the wine.

The beauty of this unpolished experience is that it can be done anywhere there is snow. It is the essential ingredient of the suppleness of skiing. If some days the preset tracks of a touring center are icy or rutty, head off the track to save the day. Being a backcountry skier also allows you to extend your season. When commercial areas shut down in the East, or the Midwest is out of snow, you'll still find great skiing on eastern ridge tops or in the Rockies, Cascades, and High Sierra far into April, May, and June.

Tactical Skiing

A few years ago, we watched Sierra guide Tom Carter bomb down Unicorn Peak in Yosemite and head for the most direct exit available: the drainage of Elizabeth Lake. Direct it was, but also steep, thick with trees, downed wood, bare spots, and gullies. Carter bushwhacked the terrain at a breakneck pace. Sun cups, logs, bare spots, and rocks were skimmed, vaulted, skirted, and shunned in an astonishing display of shoot-from-the-hip route finding.

Whether you're on an extreme mission like Carter's or on something tamer, your success in going up or down through rough terrain and different snow conditions depends on the timely use of some of the basics—the traverse, the kick turn, the sidestep, the sideslip, the herringbone, the wedge, and the straight descent. These are ways to descend at your discretion. Mastery of these simple moves, coupled with the proper instincts for when to use them, is what leading guide Allan Bard calls "tactical skiing."

"When you use a technique as a tool," says Bard, "it's a tactic." Sideslipping is a technique. Used to start a turn on a steep slope, it becomes a tactic. "Sideslip here, do a little stem

Sidehill skiing: holding an edge

christie around this rock," he says, creating a scenario. "Sideslip back in the other direction. Kick turn and traverse out. This is what comes to play in backcountry skiing. You have to start thinking a bit."

The backcountry brings you back to basics. Out there, these simple moves become focused in ways not found on groomed trails and packed slopes. A schuss on a slope presenting snow of variable consistency keeps you on your toes (or heels as it may be). Sure, you can conduct a steady traverse over the hill from the touring center, but can you do it on a thirty-degree slope? Or in crud? Or ice? You're matching your wits and your inventory of skills with wilderness. Skis are tools of travel.

The stride: Varying terrain and snow conditions are constantly playing havoc with efficient forward progress. The East even has a whimsical way to measure this frustration, known as the "Worcester Scale." It is named after the mountain range on the east side of Stowe, Vermont. The scale begins at one with machine-set tracks. Once you venture from these, you ascend the scale. Close trees and thick brush measure a six or so. Clawing your way from spruce to spruce (up or down) is around eight. At ten, forget the ski poles and bring a chain saw.

Stay low and wide in steep chutes.

Working up the Worcester Scale

New England or the Midwest calls for some impromptu and off-beat techniques. They involve plenty of twisting, pivoting, flailing, ducking, lunging, hanging on, and corkscrewing around trees. You won't find these maneuvers discussed here or elsewhere in the literature of skiing. You don't learn *how* to flail on skinny skis, you just *do* it as snow and terrain dictate. For example, when the tight lines of unyielding spruce cramp your style, and your ski poles plunge in to the handles in the tractionless fluff, just let them dangle from wrist straps and pull yourself uphill from tree to tree like a long-toed sloth.

Skiing downhill through trees may become addictive. Pole straps come off the wrists for downhill unless you want to risk the shoulder-wrenching surprise of catching your basket on a branch. In tight trees, you've got to be up on your skis and more than a little cocky. Categories of turns disappear as an up-coming maple calls for a half telemark with a skate turn followed by a jumping parallel conclusion. Call them what you will, but get around the tree.

Because of these obstacles, most instructors don't over-emphasize flawless striding form. (And if you think obstacles don't exist in the West, then spend an afternoon in a colony of sun cups, where kick and glide become pitch and yaw.) Todd Eastman says the most effective ski form is a sort of abbreviated diagonal stride, which he calls the "diagonal shuffle."

The shuffle keeps your pace quick and your options open. It also affords the kind of balance and control you need to segue into a kick turn or a sidestep; Eastman considers the latter a vital backcountry move for short, steep pitches. He doesn't recommend the conventional sidestep, but a "full-gaited" maneuver, "The Clydesdale," which clears snow off the skis instead.

"You're always coming back to the simplest thing you've learned on skis, be it a kick turn, a snowplow, or a bailout," says Eastman about backcountry skiing. "They're all in your bag of tricks."

The fall: When Bard gets down to basics, he starts simple. His prerequisite for skiing in the backcountry is "to get

A vital downhill skill: Tossing the Anchor

in and out of your skis by yourself, even in a foot of snow, having the good sense not to put your pack on first."

Of course, having to get back into skis and pack usually occurs after a fall—and everyone falls in the backcountry. But more than resigning to it, you should use it to your benefit. "The first thing you do to learn downhill skills is to sit down, bail out, and toss the anchor," says Eastman, ticking off most of the euphemisms for a strategic flop. "You've got to be able to sit down instantly—get hands and feet up." In other words, in deep snow make sure your hands and feet don't get buried, and on hard snow keep them clear so gear doesn't get too banged up.

It's a tactic, says Eastman, that shouldn't be abandoned even when you take on more difficult skiing. "When you're skiing down a wooded trail, you don't just do nice long turns. You turn where the trail turns, and do a couple of turns in between to keep your speed down," he says. "It's a game that requires quick reactions and sitting down a lot."

The ride down: Preferable to bailing out, in some instances, is simple schussing, running it straight downhill. Schussing is taught to beginners to improve balance. It's also a better, safer tactic on difficult snow than trying to turn. In fact, we sometimes don't put all that much emphasis on turning, period, which isn't surprising given the open terrain of locales like the Sierra. A more efficient downhill route can often be accomplished by traversing and sideslipping.

But what if you're not in the wide, steep bowls of the Sierra but are in eastern neighborhoods? What if you're in ex-

The backcountry can be the site of Olympic performances.

tremely tight quarters on your way down, say, a slick, skied-out trail? One way to control your speed is to get to the side and into unpacked snow that will slow you down. Or use the terrain to your advantage by skiing up into the sides of the gully, banking and turning, and heading back down and across to the other side to check speed. Otherwise expect a prolonged session of wedging.

Skiing in deeper snow—over six inches—also can make it easier to learn how to turn. We do just this with our students, instructing them to make their stances hip width as if they're going to wedge, but without toeing in. They simply steer their feet right to go right, left to go left. Easy.

For those times down, when it's still difficult to turn, consider wearing climbing skins on the bottoms of your skis. Skins are usually used only for uphills. But on the downslope, they'll slow your pace just as deeper snow does. You leave them on for the same reason you might take them off on a gentler hill or in terrain other than breakable crust: to enjoy the downhill.

In the course of any downhill run, no turn is more important than the first, for it determines rhythm, timing, and confidence. The first turn is also a chance to test the consistency of the snow. Miss it, and the run turns into a series of linked recoveries. Even if you're a parallel skier, a stem christie or stem telemark is often the perfect way to get into the game. It's very secure and controlled. If you start by schussing or jumping (bring the industrial-strength pampers), it's far more photogenic, as is the likely cartwheeling conclusion.

Traversing: Often the lay of the land or pockets of bad snow force you to traverse into the good skiing. This sideslipping across the slope gives you a chance to plumb the snow.

Whatever the angle of the slope, a sure way to tell if you're having trouble holding a steady traversing line is to look back at your tracks. If they wander, you have too much weight on your uphill ski. The ski is leading you up and making you overcompensate to get back down to the traversing line. This is a result of shoulders that are square to the skis and hands that are directly in front of your body. The remedy? Push the uphill hand forward, as if you are throwing a roundhouse. This puts more weight on the downhill ski for a straighter line, and it is also a good position from which to sideslip. Just ease pressure off the edges and let the skis slide.

But sometimes when you're traversing slippery, hard

Traversing to get down can be a technique of choice with a heavy pack.

snow, the last thing you want to do is let your edges go. Instinct tells you to grip for survival—though overedging can kick your skis loose. Lean out from the hill with your upper body so your weight is over your feet; drive your knees into the hill so your edges are useful (body position of angulation). You should *hold* the edge. Just stay on it more precisely.

When approaching a new climb, plan out the most logical route around obstacles. Instead of butting heads with the slope head on, take it at manageable angles or traverses, especially if you're carrying a heavy backpack or breaking trail in deep snow. Instead of picking the ski up at each stride, let it ride up and out of the snow. If you're reduced to a sidestep, modify your technique so you step up and forward each time. Ski smart. If you get to the top of a ridge and are too exhausted to ski down the other side, you haven't done a very good job.

Skating: Traveling in a direct, efficient manner is one good reason to try skating in the backcountry. Lakes are as much a part of the remote areas as mountains, and there is no easier way to get across them than to skate. Skating is something to be done on another plane—literally. Most skiers skate on a flat plane or an uphill or a downhill. Tilt it, too: use the technique on sidehills. Skate and step up to hold a line or gain elevation if you have some speed built up. Make the elevation work for you. Make everything work. That's the lesson you need to learn. Points are not necessarily awarded for form; it doesn't have to be pretty.

Skins: You can also traverse up small hills with the aid of climbing skins. Skiers new to these tools tend to snowshoe with them. Instead, keep as much of the skin on the snow as possible. If the slope angle is low, and the snow soft, cock your ankles and keep the full width of the skin on the snow for traction. This means keeping your knee directly over the ski instead of turned into the slope. Even on traverses with hard snow when you have to use more edge, skim the skinned-up skis along. Better yet, take the skins off so you can really edge an icy traverse.

Climbing skins give foolproof grip on sustained ascents, steep grades, and deep, rotten snow. No ski mountaineer is without them. They allow you to go straight at most hills as if you had super wax. Keep your head up so your weight stays

Ripping hides—don't bother taking off the skis to shuck skins for the descent.

over your feet, and get your shoulders into the poling. Skins save a lot of energy. As our good friend, Casey Sheahan, says, "Skins make molehills out of mountains."

How? Today's artificial sealskins are made of nylon or mohair, and they stick with adhesive to ski bottoms. Once applied, the effect is like a carpet of thousands of tiny hairs. The hairs are long enough to dig into the snow for grip, yet lie down smoothly when the ski slides forward.

Skins should be more than half the width of the ski. They stick better to a dry ski bottom. The adhesive will work for a dozen or so applications. When not using them, always fold the ends to the middle, and the sticky side back on itself to protect the adhesive. In an emergency, you can improvise climbers by braiding small-diameter rope over and under the length of the ski (in effect, putting chains on your skis).

Pack: Though you won't always need skins, you will need a pack, day variety or larger. It should fit you like your skis or boots, loosened for ease on uphills, cinched tight for the ride back. You want a rucksack that moves as if it's part of you. An ill-fitting pack is an ill-tempered brute with an independent temperament that often takes charge, directing severe head plants.

Skiing with a pack isn't necessarily difficult. But making adjustments—recovering from a sudden change in snow conditions or terrain—can be more of a problem. "People think you have to do more. Really, it's doing less," says Allan Bard, explaining that you don't have to contort your upper body to make adjustments. A slight angling of the hips is all that is necessary to pull off a turn if the weight of your pack is properly balanced.

Steep Stuff

There is no shortage of ways to test your limits on skis: marathon runs, telemark races, expeditions. Skiing extremely steep inclines is one of the big tests, but it's for only a few gutsy experts. Not only do you have to ski extreme slopes without technical mistakes, you also have to think positively before and during the descent. We like to sense a practiced confidence in our friends who ski steep inclines. So why do it? Some thrive on the giddy feeling of biting off a little more than they can chew, then pulling off the feat.

Slopes of thirty to forty degrees are very steep. All alpine skiers would agree. (Snow walls up to sixty degrees have been negotiated by specialists.) Skiing a thirty-plus-degree slope on metal-edged telemark skis is far more difficult than tackling the same slope on alpine equipment. There is less control due to the light and free-heeled skis and boots, and thus there is less of a margin for error and chance for recovery. The practical limits of downhill skiing are governed by the ability to hold a ski edge on snow. Telemark boots restrict these limits in cross-country downhill. They are more flexible than their alpine cousins. On the steep, great muscular tension is demanded to hold an edge. The telemark boot simply will not do as much work for you as will an alpine boot.

To complete a descent that has never been done or done only on alpine skis is to meet a wonderful challenge. This is called a first descent. It is a gold-medal performance.

Aside from choosing the right stable snow conditions for the job, the main problem in extreme skiing is controlling the wild acceleration that occurs when you point your skis down the fall line. It calls for sharp powerful turns, linked one on top of the other, that bring your skis back to the horizontal before you gain too much speed. You need to exaggerate the quickness of your best parallel skiing into a repeated short-swing rhythm. (Telemarks are more vulnerable here. If you insist on tellies in steep, hard snow, step around smartly, but return to the more stable position between turns. Do this by doing early lead-ski changes.)

A strong edge set is critical at the end and beginning of each turn, when your skis are across the slope and nearly stopped. Slam those super-flexed knees quickly into the hill to set your edges. Look downhill to anticipate and plant your pole. The rebound off the edge set gives you total unweighting to pivot your skis in an airy swing from left to right, then back. In this kind of fall-away steepness, the start of the turn looks like a jump, but is more a delicate step out over the space below. Land on flexed knees, ready for the next turn. On extreme terrain, even good skiers often sideslip into each turn, especially the first.

You may sideslip a long way before collecting yourself enough to make that first pivot, as Gillette and Art Burrows did starting down the U-Notch in the Palisades of California's Sierra Nevada. This was a first cross-country descent of a couloir that is classified as a moderate ice climb in the summer. It runs near forty degrees with a little stint of forty-five degrees at the very

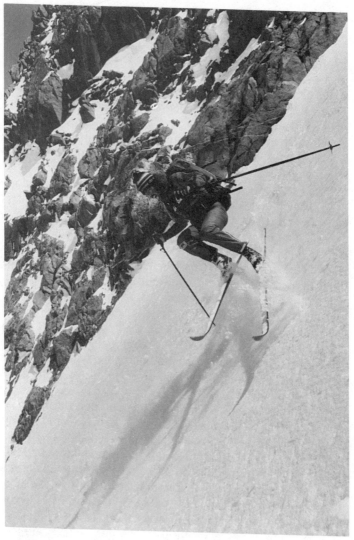

Art Burrows in the U-Notch

top. Here the boys were seen gingerly creeping sideways, stealing rather than skiing some vertical, their uphill hands dragging the snow. Nothing fancy, but concentrated. Extreme skiing is a matter of mind set as much as edge set.

Below, the snowy runnel widened as if it had pushed aside the rocky walls. The angle eased to maybe thirty-eight degrees. As the snow softened enough to take an edge, the boys hardened, and skied, ecstatic, with no thought of falling. What a ride. This was no place for long, drawn-out telemarks. Rapid-fire survival parallels were in order. Skis swung across the elevator-shaft steepness, committing their riders to a weightless freedom unknown on moderate slopes. Toward the bottom, weightlessness went whacky. Airborne Art flew across the bergschrund—ten feet up. He touched down, bumped and swerved, and, dropping into long telemarks, taxied out onto the Palisade Glacier apron.

Sometimes you want to go one step further, which may be close to one step too far. On another first nordic descent, this time of an entire mountain, only a skier's self-arrest—a technique of last resort—worked. After climbing up the Polish Glacier with crampons, Gillette and Pete Patterson (fourth in the 1980 Olympic downhill) stood at the top of Argentina's Aconcagua—at 22,834 feet, the highest peak in the western hemisphere. They put on telemark skis, and each lashed an ice axe to the handle of a ski pole for self arrest in case of an uncontrolled fall. They eased down the summit ridge, descended the upper glacier, and threaded their way through the crevasse band.

Below lay a thousand feet of mixed ice, bullet-proof firn snow and, thankfully, tiny islands of wind-blown snow. The trick was to go for the safe islands, and turn on edgeable snow. The wide telemark skis were at their limits. Alpine skis would have been better, but they were trying something new.

Gillette, turning out of a Vermont milk-stool squat position, blew it, fell, and stopped himself. Pete, expertly aggressive, stabbed into punched turns. Suddenly he fell, hard. On the slick surface, his speed translated directly into an out-of-control, wild slide. Gillette watched, terrified. It looked like a grotesque road-runner cartoon—a barreling cloud of kicked-up snow hurtling downhill, straight toward a plunge over a series of small ice walls. It seemed inevitable. But Pete got his ice axe, always ready, into position and hung on in a self-arrest. The pick finally dug in. He stopped three-hundred feet down, just short of the ice walls. Gillette skittered down to him, untangled skis and poles, arms and legs. Together they sidled the final vertical down to their high camp and brewed tea.

Ruling Unruly Snow

Skiing through fluff or on a packed avenue is easy. The challenge lies in the stages of snow in between powder and packed. Here your center of balance and the speed you carry are critical. Honing technique to ski lousy snow makes you a complete skier.

Pushing the limits of the herringbone

Avalanche Gulch runs 6,000 vertical feet down the volcanic cone of northern California's 14,162-foot Mount Shasta. Hard, wind-packed snow, unyielding as macadam, paved the steep upper slopes on the May day that Gillette and friends tackled it. But farther down, the sun had mixed a potpourri of sugar and mush. Top and bottom called for completely different parallel and telemark strategies. You need more than one kind of turn to handle the steep and deep, the crud and trees, the narrow and icy. As terrain, snow, and speed vary, you even need different types of parallels and telemarks.

Easterner Todd Eastman, displaying a flamboyant disregard for textbook turns, insists his real learning occurs between head plants in horrific snow while skiing home from work in the dark. Westerner Steve Barnett says, "Always try every terrain, every snow. Never back off. You'll always learn something, and grin crazily at the bottom."

Ice and hard snow: Even with metal-edged cross-country skis, biting into the concrete-hard snow at the top of Avalanche Gulch was extremely difficult. You'll find the same conditions at touring centers on icy klister days with plastic-bottomed track skis. Expect greater than the normal amount of wild sliding and skidding. New skis, with acute right-angle edges not yet worn down, help tremendously. If you have metal edges for true cross-country downhill, sharpen them for better hold. Torsionally stiff boots are great for control.

On very hard snow, a parallel turn is best, or, as a next resort, a stem christie. Forgo telemarks. Gillette opted for parallel turns on the top of Mount Shasta. It is easier to bite with both skis parallel, easier to get around through the fall line quickly, and, most critical, easier to brake speed with heel checks. The key is exerting pressure on that downhill ski—standing on that edge. Dramatic angulation and thrusting your knees into the hill ensure a trusty edge hold. Remember to keep your upper body leaning away from the slope so that your weight is directly over your skis throughout turns. Many telemaniacs do adapt tellies to firm snow by using lots of angulation, but tellies are not at their best here.

The true telemark is a banked turn with a lot of lean, making it easy to lose your edges on hard pack. If you genuflect, be careful to keep weight on your rear ski so both will carve and hold. A step telemark, which gets you around quickly, is likely to force too much weight onto the front ski. On hard snow, the practical slope angle for effective telemarking is more moderate than in softer conditions. Too much speed is gained in the long sweep through the fall line. Art Burrows says, "I ski with my feet closer together in a hard-packed telemark, really a half parallel and half telly. In this way I get more equal pressure on both legs. It's easier to press on the rear ski and get a quicker edge change."

Ski edges grabbing and letting go with staccato chattering? It's due to too much edge. Get on and off your edges more quickly. You'll find skidding is often necessary to slow down on ice. To avoid chattering, edge the ski, less acutely at first but progressively more through the turn. Chattering is a sure sign that either you're leaning too much into the turn (banking) or that your boots are torsionally too flexible, allowing the ski to flutter.

When you get into trouble on hardpack, immediately assume a parallel stance. But in powder, a telemark stance gives stability in tight situations.

Icing: Cross-country skiing is often frustrated by peculiar snow conditions that build up ice on ski bottoms. This usually occurs at that temperature most dreaded by skiers, thirty-two degrees Fahrenheit (zero degrees centigrade), when no wax seems to work, and waxless skis clump up with snow. To prevent the warm air from warming the ski base, thus making it more prone to icing, keep your skis pressed on the ground and sliding at all times; if you stop, move your feet in place.

Late in the winter when the sun is high, or in the Sierra of California, a new fall of powder snow gets worked over by the sun very quickly. The top inch or two of snow gets soggy, yet underneath is dry powder. The trick for minimizing icing here is to keep your skis deep under the snow where it's consistently cold. Don't pick up your skis and collect surface moisture.

The sun also melts the snow on trees, dripping and causing wet areas beneath. Double-pole through these areas, then continue pressing your skis on the ground after you get back into the dryer snow to sponge off the moisture they picked up.

When skiing through the Brooks Range in 1972, Gillette and his companions traveled mostly on frozen rivers. But the rivers were not always completely frozen! Often a thin layer of water—called "overflow"—lurked beneath the surface snow that covered the river. If they were quick enough, they could ski through it, then right on into the super-dry snow of Arctic

Perfect snow—roll your own.

Alaska, wiping the moisture off on the dry absorbent powder without losing a stride.

The easiest way to remove accumulated ice from ski bases without taking off your skis is to scrape one ski back and forth over the other just in front of the binding. Or scrape over a branch that is lying in the trail.

Deep powder: When it comes to powder poaching, cross-country downhill can be just as much fun as alpine. Both parallels and telemarks work, although here the telly, being a steered turn, is truly in its element. You'll have more fun than a gopher in soft dirt.

The first ingredient for handling powder is accepting some speed. Speed allows you to lean into a deep-snow telemark, working against a "bank" of snow. Refusal to sign this contract with gravity is the greatest psychological barrier to becoming a powder hound. You have to point them down the hill and let them run, then ride them. And you have to get used to losing sight of your skis in the deep stuff.

Maintain rhythm. Think of sliding that front telemark ski forward like the repeated pattern of your diagonal stride. The "set" at the end of one turn is the start of the next. Planting the

219

pole is optional. Breaking this rhythm with long traverses between turns kills timing. When skiing well, you'll find you don't pull out of your rhythm when in trouble but crank into another turn for your recovery. The ability to recover is the key to cross-country downhill.

Establishing one long platform on which the skis are kept evenly weighted will let your skis plane, or float, the easier to turn. Too much weight on a single ski submerges it. Squeeze that rear ski through with a steady pressure to change lead between turns and don't bob up and down. This smooth cruise makes telemarking ideal for toting backpacks on loose-heeled equipment.

Parallel turns use the same principles of speed, rhythm, and equal weighting of the skis to establish a strong platform from which to work in powder. Ride a cushion of snow with little edging, but instead of banking into the turns, stay pretty much directly over your skis with your feet together. In the turn, draw your knees up, let your ski tails "stall" down into the snow, then let your tips fall off into the turn. Severe unweighting is called for, but just in your knees; the upper body stays neutral. Rick Barker snorts, "I get low enough so I can smell my feet. I get down like I positioned myself in my surfing days. That centers me over my skis, instituting control. Then I just roll my knees into and out of each turn."

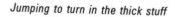

Jumping to turn in the thick stuff

Crud: Most skiers don't want to tackle slush, mush, Sierra cement, or mashed potato snow on three-pin equipment. But when nature dumps, and you're due out of the backcountry for a Monday morning appearance at the office, read on to pick up techniques of salvage more glorious than carving zorros (the kick turn and traverse of last resort).

When the crud is merely extremely heavy powder, you can still steer and ride your skis around in an ordinary telemark. It is a valuable energy-conserving technique, but you've got to customize it to the conditions. It is not such a fluid process as in light powder. Since the snow is dense, once you get your skis turning, they'll "catch" and whip around. The key is starting the turn. From a definite set at the end of the turn, rise up definitely and unweight during the lead change. Sometimes a double-pole plant helps this launching process; this releases your skis from the grip of gravity and snow to steer into the next turn. Sink and press down and around in the turn. Exaggerate the definite rise up and lunge downward to obtain power. Keep a lot of weight on the rear ski, then turn with even pressure so you don't sink the front ski and throw yourself off balance.

To ski crud in a parallel, crouch to stabilize yourself. To initiate each turn, thrust your heels down, unweight, then drastically roll your knees into the turn to steer and press the skis around with great compression. Think of almost pushing both feet downhill ahead of yourself. Extending them like this, add strength through the turn. Feel a lot of twisting in the stomach muscles, almost as if you were throwing the skis in the other direction. Avoid the tendency to initiate each turn by jumping erratically off staccato pole plants. Stem christies are trusty allies here. Even snowplows.

When the snow hardens almost to cement, truly radical unweighting is called for. This means you have to get up and out of the snow to steer around. Telemarking still? Initiate the turn with a step up and around the fall line with the forward ski, thus avoiding the vicelike grip of the mush. Or step all the way through the fall line with two steps by taking the first step with the downhill ski, the next with the uphill, then sink into your telly. Step, step, telly. A low telemark is a strong, stable position for bad snow. It doesn't matter so much what happens to you between stable positions, just get from one stable position to the next.

You can also simply jump your skis up and out of the

Adjust technique to fickle backcountry snow.

snow from one parallel stance one hundred and eighty degrees across the hill to the other direction. Going weightless. Gorilla turns. Again, it doesn't matter what happens in the air, only on the landing, a decidedly flexed-knee affair.

Crust and wind slab: These are the nastiest of all snow conditions. Crust is usually formed by freezing temperatures after sun or rain; wind slab results from high winds packing the surface. Underlying both, lurking as in ambush, can be soft snow. Here skiing is stop and go.

If you're faced with a downhill section, any one of a number of turns might work. One thing is for certain: you'll have to ease into them, skiing with real delicacy and poise so you'll skitter over the crust. If the crust refuses to support your weight, your only alternative is to resort to wild step turns, slow stem christies, step telemarks, or traverses and kick turns, and accept your education as it comes. Slow snowplows often are best. This is no time for bravado. Ice crust can cut shins. Windslab can "dinner plate" away underneath your skis, sending you plummeting.

Galen Rowell's
unique method
of stopping in
windblown,
crusty snow

CHAPTER 13

Adventure Skiing with Ned Gillette

I began skiing at the age of three—1948. I was new and so was the sport. I was small, and the mountains were big. As I grew, the mountains seemed to shrink. Skiing became civilized. Something was missing—something beautiful and exotic and free with a measure of uncertainty. I felt a need to put excitement back into my skiing. That's when adventure skiing was created; imaginative explorations with small, fast, self-sufficient teams on skis with free-heeled bindings.

My teams rummaged through the world's great mountain ranges, always on the go like gypsies. Skis were our passports into seldom-traveled lands. As the late British mountaineer, Eric Shipton, wrote, ". . . to become an expert in any field, however outlandish, can open the most unexpected doors." At a time when I was hearing that little new adventure remained, it was a chance to pioneer, or shall I say re-pioneer (after Nansen and Amundsen). Today there is still plenty left to do; we just have to use our imaginations.

For me, major-league adventure skiing started in 1972 as part of a team that crossed Alaska's Brooks Range. Now I've skied on all seven continents. The big expeditions are blow-out challenges. They're satisfying in a hard, goal-oriented way. But the ski jaunts that replenish the spirit are the small ones: rocketing runs chasing hooligan powder poachers down trails like the abandoned Teardrop on Mt. Mansfield; backdoor tours through Percy's Vermont sugarbush; spring tours in the Sierra sun. On fat skis, on skinny skis. As adventure ski guide, Allan Bard,

Ruth Glacier on Mt. McKinley

Brooks Range, Alaska, 1972

says, "The place you choose and the tools you use are up to you. It's all skiing."

Allan goes on about the fact that you don't have to travel thousands of miles or spend a lot of money for adventure skiing. He lives at the foot of the Sierra. "When we saw some of the skiing right here in our backyard, it was like a door opened—a plum waiting to be plucked. We said, 'Why not, and if why not, why not us? Here's our own golden age. We can try things that have never been done and maybe show some people that this kind of skiing is possible.'"

Brooks Range, Alaska, 1972: The Brooks Range stretches six hundred miles across northern Alaska. Rivers run wild for their full course through a splendid land of varied wild-life. In 1972, before the oil pipeline was pushed through, it was probably the final section of the United States unchanged from its wilderness birth.

Wayne Merry, Jack Miller, Jed Williamson, and I skied across it in thirty days: up the North Fork of the Koyukuk River through the Gates of the Arctic National Park and Preserve, then down the Itkillik River to the North Slope. We used wooden Bonna 2400 skis with a cable binding. We had custom-made equipment; there was no specialized ski touring gear around in those days.

This was my first long trip. The first day, busting trail through knee-deep depth hoar under seventy-pound packs and the minus thirty-five-degree evening, quickly eroded my romantic notions of expeditions. But I learned to remember only the good times: like a hot cup of tea in cold hands, shared camaraderie, and especially the airdrop of warm chocolate chip cookies from a friend's Cessna.

Saint Elias Mountains, Alaska and Canada, 1975: The St. Elias Mountains, with Mount Logan at 19,850 feet, are split on their long axis by a series of huge ice-filled valleys. Craig Patterson, Steve Darrow, and I followed a 220-mile traverse from the Chitina River across the Bagley and Seward ice fields to Kluane Lake. The ice fields were one gorgeous ski run, but regularly interrupted by fierce storms.

In those days, we were still cutting our teeth, finding out about snowy travel, and building confidence. I had skied in Europe, but this was different. Alaska and northern Canada—distant yet familiar, grand in scale yet inexpensive—were perfect testing grounds. This was our first experiment with self-sufficiency. By hauling six-foot sleds, we were able to go all the way unsupported by food caches or airdrops. We felt like a trio of Davids going after Goliath.

Around Mount McKinley, Alaska, 1978: At 20,320 feet, Mount McKinley is the highest peak in North America. Five interconnecting glaciers form a ninety-mile ring around the peak.

Mt. St. Elias, Alaska

Mt. McKinley, Alaska, 1978

We looked at the geography and decided that, instead of going up the mountain like everybody else, we'd go around it. Galen Rowell, Allan Bard, Doug Wiens, and I accidentally invented a new sport called "orbiteering" or going around things.

There were two big problems. First, the glaciers were divided by high passes that demanded technical climbing with crampons and ice axes. Second, our sponsorship entailed testing the new fifty-millimeter racing binding. Sometimes, under heavy packs, we were as goofy as drunken sailors on the light equipment. But, in nineteen days, we made it up the Kahiltna Glacier, down the Peters Glacier, up the Traleika Glacier, through the Ruth Glacier, and down the East Fork Glacier—all in splendid scenery of Himalayan majesty.

Later, in a climb more exhausting than seemed possible, Galen and I made a one-day ascent of McKinley. That had never been done before.

High Arctic, Ellesmere Island, Canada, 1977: This was the big one after five years of developing winter travel expertise, and it was the first time we raised cash sponsorship. Doug Wiens, Allan Bard, Chuck Schultz, and I went as far north as land allows—eighty-three degrees latitude—and skied

Ellesmere Island, Canadian Arctic, 1977

around the northern portion of Ellesmere Island. It is a land of staggering beauty and solitude and surprisingly rich wildlife. Robert Peary departed for the North Pole from Ellesmere.

Our 450-mile trip took fifty-two days. For the first time, we used fiberglass skis, but only forty-seven-millimeters wide. We

Eve Icefall, New Zealand Alps

Karakoram, Himalaya, Pakistan

were self-sufficient, solving the problem of carrying all food and gear by lugging eight-foot sleds. Each man's sled weighed 240 pounds when we started from Lake Hazen. Chuck named his sled "Hemorrhoid." The first day we covered a meager four miles and camped exhausted. Wrestling chaotic ocean ice pressure ridges on the Robeson Channel forced us to get tough. On 5 May, the lads laid on a surprise birthday party for me, complete with party favors. Later, herds of musk ox and arctic wolves greeted us before we climbed over the Grant Ice Cap.

Southern Alps, New Zealand, 1979: Distance in the Southern Alps is different: miles are nothing, it is the weather and vertical that give you a devastating run for your money. While chasing winter down under, Allan Bard, Tom Carter, Jan Reynolds, and I required thirty-two days to go ninety miles through the mountains north of Mount Cook to the Rakaia River.

Although the trip was planned as a holiday, it turned out to be an epic. We climbed up and telemarked down over twenty thousand vertical feet, had avalanches nipping at our heels, forded endless rivers, bushwhacked through jungles, and spent over half the days marooned in huts or tents or snow caves. At one point we were pinned down for seven days, all four of us in a single two-person VE-24 tent with only two days of rations. All that simply made the sparkling days in places like the Garden of Eden more valued.

Across the Karakoram, Pakistan, 1980: The foothills of the Karakoram are home to the Baltis, a fiercely independent people. K2, the world's second-highest mountain, lies to the north among high peaks of savage beauty. Galen Rowell, Kim Schmitz, Dan Asay, and I completed a six-week, 285-mile traverse during late winter. We were the first expedition to move under its own power through the heart of the Karakoram. Our dogleg route from the Indian border nearly to the Afghanistan border followed four huge glaciers: the Siachen, Baltoro, Biafo, and Hispar.

This was the most grueling of all the expeditions. In the winter of 1980, we were the only expedition in the entire Karakoram. To be self-sufficient, we each lugged 120 pounds. At one point, we climbed on nordic skis to 22,500 feet to traverse the south face of Sia Kangri. Temperatures sometimes swung one-hundred degrees from day to night. When we finished at Hunza, we'd each lost 25 pounds.

The danger of an expedition like this is different than that of a climbing foray. Here, danger lay in something going wrong

Muztagata, Western China, 1980

Everest Grand Circle, Tibet, 1982

in remote country with no chance of outside rescue.

Muztagata, Western China, 1980: This was the end of the search for the one truly great run on the perfect big skiing mountain. To find it, Galen Rowell, Jan Reynolds, and I had to go to the far west of China, beyond the Silk Road city of Kashi (Kashgar), where East first met West two thousand years ago. From there, following Marco Polo's route, we traveled into the High Pamirs, "The Roof of the World," where Kirgiz nomads roam. We were the first Americans to climb in China in forty-eight years.

Camels served as porters moving our gear up to 17,000 feet on Muztagata, "Father of the Ice Mountains." Using alpine touring gear, we skied in stages upward to the summit, climbing nearly 5,000 feet from our high camp the last day. For us, the descent was the ultimate prize as we plunged through great gulps of vertical in eight inches of light snow, golden in fading light as the sun settled over Russia. Jan set the woman's high-altitude skiing record of 24,757 feet.

Everest Grand Circle, Nepal and Tibet, 1981–1982:

Everest, the "third pole," is still the ultimate lodestone for mountaineers. While most climbers seek new ways to gain the summit, Jan Reynolds and I looked at this old subject from a different perspective. We tackled it horizontally instead of vertically and became the first team to circle the mountain. Since Everest sits astride a closed border, we broke our trip into two halves, thus visiting two exotic cultures. Our orbit took four months and covered three hundred miles.

As a novel way to touch the border and begin the Nepal leg, we climbed Pumori, a 23,442-foot pyramid. Jim Bridwell led the route. It was the first winter ascent by Americans in the Himalaya. Then we swung south around Everest by climbing over three 20,000-foot passes. We ran out of food for five days during the hike out to our sherpas. Later, in Tibet, we retraced the footsteps of the original 1921 British reconnaisance expedition and had a chance to telemark in the shadow of Everest. The final mark of success was returning better friends than when we left.

Aconcagua, Argentina, 1984

Aconcagua, Argentina, 1984: By 1984, I figured I'd better knock off the remaining continents that presented unique skiing opportunities. Aconcagua, 22,834 feet, is the highest peak in the Western Hemisphere. I planned to make the first telemark ski descent. I teamed up with Pete Patterson, an ex-alpine ski teamer, who had placed fourth in the 1980 Olympic downhill. Using crampons, we climbed the Polish Glacier. At the summit, we put on skis.

The upper ridges and slopes were fun. But as we dropped lower, the glacial surface became hideous—half ice and half windslab. We skittered and rasped back and forth, on the edge of control. I fell, recovered. Suddenly Pete fell hard, plummeting three-hundred feet before stopping himself with his ice axe on the edge of a small ice cliff. Together we negotiated the final vertical, shaky but happy to have survived, and satisfied.

Mountains of the Moon, Zaire and Uganda, 1985: The Ruwenzori, the fabled "Mountains of the Moon," lie on the border between Zaire and Uganda and rise to 16,763 feet. The paradoxical range lies almost on the equator, yet bears permanent snow and glaciers. I wanted to go there because of reports of plants gone crazy, growing ten times their normal height; mountain gorillas; elephant-related animals that shriek at night, and the ski club of Uganda. Eligibility requirement? Ski the Ruwenzori. So I did.

After adventures typical of a first timer in Africa, I managed to find the mountains, hire a Zairois guide and porters, and trek three days from Mutwanga to the edge of the snow. The guides waved goodbye. Racing deteriorating weather, I climbed solo up Margherita, the highest peak, then hitched on my telemark skis and swished down beautiful corn snow on the Stanley ice cap. I had joined the Uganda Ski Club.

Antarctica, 1987: Antarctica was my seventh and final continent. I skied it while on a reconnaisance trip to prepare to row a specially designed boat from Cape Horn to the Antarctic Peninsula. The next year I returned south to complete our attempt to row to Antarctica. Departing into a raging fifty knot gale which capsized us three times, we persisted through frigid conditions and arrived two weeks later. This extraordinary expedition left me smoothly elated to have, once again, pushed beyond our normal limits.

Index

Adventure skiing 225–35
Avalanches 189–93
Backcountry skiing 195–222
  survival skills 178–93
Body position 66–67, 98–101
Boots and bindings 121–25
  seventy-fives 122–23
  skating 124–25
  systems 124
Children, teaching 157–63
Christies 77–80
  sideslip 79
  stem 97
Citizen racing 167–72
Clothing 131–37
Cold, coping with 183–89
Crud 221–22
Crust and wind slab 222
Diagonal stride 19–21, 47
Downhill skiing 63–93,
  212–15
Edges 76–77, 119
Equipment 115–37, 162,
  181–82
  repairs 182–83
Falling 15, 89–90, 208
  getting up 68–69
Flat terrain skiing 19–33

Herringboning 35–37
Hypothermia 188–89
Ice 217–18
Icing 218–19
Kick 20, 32–33
Kick turn 38–39
Layering, 132, 133–34
Learning, attitude 14–17
  for downhill skiers 22–23
Marathon skate 53–55
Moguls 109–10
Packs 127–30, 212
Parallel turn 81–83, 85–87,
  220, 221
Poles 22, 32, 125–127
Poling 25–33, 87–89,
  101–102
  double 31–32
  grip 27, 28
  kick double 32–33
  power 30–31
Powder, deep 219–20
Racing 112–13, 167–75
  citizen 167–72
  training 172–75
Rilling 150–52
Roller skiing 174
Seniors, skiing for 163–65

Sideslipping 76–77
Sidestepping 37
Skate, diagonal or
  herringbone 56
  marathon 53–55
  V-1 48–53
  V-2 55–56
Skating 43–61
  boots 124–25
  free 58
  jump 56–58
  on differing snows 58–59
  poles 126
  skis 120
  uphill 59–61
Skiing, downhill 63–93,
  212–15
  flat terrain 19–33
  steep slopes 212–15
  tactical 202–12
  tandem 40–41
  uphill 33–35, 211–12
Skins, climbing 211–12
Skis, 116–21
  bags 131
  fitting 120–21
  repair 183
  skating 120
  waxless 22, 117–18
Sleds 130
Snow conditions 216–22
  crud 221–22
  crust and wind slab 222
  ice 217–18
  icing 218–19
  powder, deep 219–20
Speeding 89, 112
Stem christie 79

Stop, hockey 80–81
  wedge 72–73
Straight run 67–68
Strides, diagonal 19–21
  slippery 24–25
Striding 19–25
Sun, protection from 136–37
Survival skills 177–93
  shelter, providing 184–85
Tacking 37–38
Telemark 95–113, 217, 221
  body position 98–101
  racing 112–13
  step 108–10
  wedge 107–108
Terrain, coping with 202–215
Traversing 37, 209–10
Turns, kick 38–39
  linking 83–87, 110
  parallel 81–83, 85–87,
    220, 221
  skate 70
  stem christie 79
  step 69–71
  telemark 95–113, 217, 221
  wedge 74–76
Uphill skiing 33–35, 211–12
V-1 skate 48–53
V-2 skate 55—56
Waxes 139–55
  application 142–44,
    146–47, 148–49
  glide 148–55
  grip 140–47
  removal 145
Waxing 139–55
Wedging 72–74
Weight shift 24, 70–71

PHOTO CREDITS

All photos by Ned Gillette except the following:

Allan Bard — Pages 128, 203
Michael Brady — Page 196 Top
Will Brewster — Pages 119, 121-23, 127
Bjorn Finstad — Page 131
John Fuller — Page 199
Paul Gallaher — Pages 12, 96, 104, 156, 169, 171
Bruce Lindwall — Pages 46, 166
Barbara Lloyd — Pages 77-78
Wayne Merry — Pages 133, 184
Peter Miller — Pages 14, 21, 28, 30-31, 36, 38-42, 44, 47, 66, 69, 71, 73, 76, 87-88, 116, 138, 142-43, 149, 159, 161, 196 Bottom, 211
Doug Weins — Page 158
Ted Wood — Page 137
Bob Woodward — Pages 142-43, 151, 155
Deborah Zarate — Page 91
Photo on page 4 courtesy of Telemark Lodge, Cable, Wisconsin
Photos on page 150 courtesy of Swix Sport
Simian one-piece suit on page 20 courtesy of John Wheeler, The Ski Rack, Burlington, Vermont.

Publisher's Note: *The presence in this book of photographs showing particular brands of skis, waxes, and other cross-country skiing gear does not constitute an endorsement of those products by The Mountaineers. The fact that particular brands are shown is incidental to the informational purposes of the photographs. Other brands would have served as well for those purposes.*

Ned Gillette (left) and John Dostal

ABOUT THE AUTHORS

Ned Gillette, headquartered in Sun Valley, Idaho, and a former member of the U.S. Olympic Ski Team has, directed ski schools in Vermont, Colorado and California. One of America's best known spokesmen on outdoor sports, he has led adventure skiing expeditions on all seven continents. Changing arenas, he also has made a daring voyage by ocean-rowing boat from Cape Horn to Antarctica. A photojournalist who writes for *National Geographic* and other magazines, he is co-author of *Everest Grand Circle* (The Mountaineers), the account of a climbing-skiing adventure in Nepal and Tibet.

John Dostal, a resident of Stowe, Vermont, has been an instructor and ski school director for 15 years, most recently at Vermont's Trapp Family Lodge. He has been an editor at a number of skiing magazines and is currently Technical Editor at *Skiing Magazine.*